Brother Harold

To Jerry Phillips
My Special Friend
in the Lord

Harold Witmer

A Living Legend
Of Faith In Action

Joe Garner Turman

©Joe Turman 2013

All rights reserved. No part of this book may be repro-
duced by any form with mechanical, photocopy, audio, ect
without written consent from the publsiher or the author.

ISBN   978-1-940725-03-1

Truth Book Publishers
824 Bills Rd
Franklin, IL 62638
877-649-9092
www.truthbookpublishers.com

First Printing 2013
Second Printng 2014
Third Printing 2014
Fourth Printing 2014

Printed in the United States of America

TRUTH BOOK PUBLISHERS

Expressions of Praise and Endorsement

At the age of 15, I had the honor and privilege of meeting Harold Witmer. After 44 years, Harold is still on fire for Christ. His life has touched not only my life, but hundreds of others around the world. His life story is an inspiration for all of us.

Dr. Richard Worsham
Founder and CEO, Military R&R Solutions,INC.

The life and work of Brother Harold Witmer is a genuine work of our Lord. He has the lost world in his heart and the hand of God upon his life. The Gospel of Christ is his passion and strength. Read and be blessed!

Dr. Roger P. Freeman
Pastor (Retired), First Baptist Church, Clarksville, TN

This powerful story of Brother Harold Witmer will bless and encourage you in your walk with the Lord. I am thankful the Lord allowed me to know and to work with this spiritual giant.

Steve Robinson
Director, Nashville/Middle TN, Fellowship of Christian Athletes

Brother Harold Witmer is a piece of work! His personality, passion and the general way he operates and lives life is on the edge, unique and powerful. Jesus has taken this man and has done a mighty work in his life, using him greatly in the Kingdom. Brother Harold's life motivated me to want to join him in handing out Bibles in Russia, so I could learn to walk with Jesus. What a privilege! Read and be blessed!

Dr. Hal Haddon
Founder and CEO, Christian Leadership Concepts (CLC)

Joe Garner Turman's book about the life and witness of Brother Harold Witmer epitomizes the statement that "God desires our availability more than our ability." Brother Harold has always been available to live out God's call in his life.

Bill Graham,
North American Mission Board, Church Planter, Pastor

I was blessed to go to Russia with my friend Brother Harold Witmer in 1998. Watching Brother Harold wait on the Lord, as numerous obstacles arose, taught me to let go and let God have His way. Brother Harold is a man of great faith who gives God all the glory. His story will bless you!

Bill Harrison
Insurance Executive
FCA Character Coach

Brother Harold Witmer's daily living by faith proved to me that God is a living God and is actively working in His and Faye's life. You will be blessed and encouraged by reading his life story.

James A. LaBrec
Senior Solutions 65

Brother Harold Witmer is one of the behind the scenes men who has truly impacted the city of Clarksville. He works tirelessly to bring glory to God without being noticed. This book will bless you.

J.C. Davis
Church Leader, Lay Speaker

Brother Harold has the unique ability to witness to all kinds of people. He is unpretentious and without guile. Persons like him come along once in a life-time. I am fortunate to call him "my friend."

Dr. John Laida
Pastor (Emeritus), First Baptist Church, Clarksville, TN

Brother Harold offers a powerful insight on faith in God and His Word. Harold's faith in God enabled him to experience "Truck" loads of miracles!

Dwight Dickson
Independent Insurance Agent

Some people might say that good things just happen around Harold Witmer; however, good things happen to those who love the Lord and are called according to His purpose. There is no question that Brother Harold loves the Lord and has stepped up to his calling to do God's work. I am proud to call Brother Harold my friend in the Lord and always appreciate his kindness and simplicity of what it means to be a doer of the Word.

Dan Calderon
Owner/GM, WCKV-TV, Clarksville, TN

Harold Witmer's story is one of the most unique in this generation. Only God could have taken a young man from the farm fields of Pennsylvania and made him counselor to and confidant of some of the world's most powerful and influential people. Harold's is a story that must be read. It will bring inspiration and hope to all who do.

Dr. Bill Shade
Director, CEO, Source of Light

Brother Harold is one of the most profound Christian men I have ever known. His faith and prayers have inspired me more than words can ever express. He is a man who does not walk in fear, but has unbelievable courage. He is a man of compassion and forgiveness. You will benefit from reading his story. It will inspire you!

Kevin C. Kennedy
The Kennedy Law Firm, PLLC

From the time I met him at Ft. Campbell in 1955, Harold has never looked back on his commitment to Christ. Where he is, God shows up and works His will through this human conduit. Read and be challenged by a simple man who believes in a great God.

Pastor Jerry Heflin, Pastor
Eastland Heights Baptist Church, Springfield, Tennessee

I was a member of the First Christian Church when Brother Harold came into Brother Bill's office and talked to him about the new birth in Jesus. I don't know all that happened, but I do know that from that day on, Brother Bill Corley, our pastor, was a new man and very excited about Jesus. I was chairman of the deacons, and I began to work with Brother Bill and other interested men in our church, in bringing the lost to Jesus. Not long after that, Brother Bill and Brother Harold, along with other men in Clarksville, felt led to start Community Church. The Lord opened the way for us to get the land and build the building. I helped build the baptismal pool and my son was the first one baptized in it. Praise the name of Jesus! He's coming soon! Read this book and be blessed!

T.L. Brewster, Deacon,
Community Church, Clarksville, Tennessee

I have known Harold & Faye Witmer since 1969. It has been a real joy to have been in many services with Brother Harold. I established First Assembly of God in Clarksville, Tennessee in 1966. Harold has been such a close friend. I served on his board at "youth challenge center" in Clarksville. He is a man of faith, he gets the job done while others are thinking about it. What a man of faith. Faye has been the wind in his sails. What a great family.

Billy R. Jones
Paster Emeritus

"Brother Harold has led a most remarkable life. The story describing his life is one of the most inspiring books I have ever read. I have personally served God since 1973 traveling around much of the world sharing my faith. After reading Brother Harold's testimony, I called him up to tell him that when I grow up, I want to be like him. His life story will help your life be drawn closer to Jesus.

Randy Weiss
President, CrossTalk International
Board Member, National Broadcaster Board

"I started with Brother Harold fifty years ago serving together on the Board of Youth Challenge. Now I am serving as Chairman of the Board at Community Church where Brother Harold is the Pastor. Brother Bill Corley preceded Brother Harold as Pastor. When Brother Bill was in the last moments of his life, he told me and others that he wanted Brother Harold to succeed him as Pastor of Community Church. Brother Bill said that Brother Harold could do it, and he has more than lived up to Brother Bill's expectations. He can take any project that comes his way, and God blesses a thousand times over. Brother Harold has been the pastor of Community Church for six years, and his ministry has blessed my life. I credit my spiritual growth to both Brother Bill Corley and to Brother Harold Witmer.

Davis Lee Potts
Chairman of the Board, Community Church
Clarksville, TN

"Over sixty years ago, I first met Brother Harold. As a new believer, he was passionate about the Gospel. His passion has continued unabated. To many who read this book, the miracles recorded here may seem to be just coincidences. Having known Brother Harold over these many years, I recognize them as "divine coincidences" similar to the life of George Mueller of Bristol, England, as he, by faith, cared for thousands of orphans. Those of us who are privileged to know Brother Harold might recognize him as the George Mueller of our day."

John Phelan
Board Member, Horton Haven Christian Camp

"I first met Brother Harold in 1969 at Youth Challenge Center in 1969. I witnessed some of the things mentioned in this book. I can tell you that although some of them are almost unbelievable, they are typical of Harold Witmer. Many of the things that Brother Harold has done and has asked God for would be considered, by some, as unbelievable. But with Brother Harold's relationship with God, nothing is impossible. Brother Harold has

Brother Harold

led hundreds of people to Christ by one on one witnessing. He taught us at Youth Challenge how to share the Gospel and sent us out to share Jesus. It was Brother Harold who taught me the meaning of "in faith, believing." He taught us that we can believe God for anything and he demonstrated that belief in his own personal life. Many of these principles that Brother Harold taught and demonstrated are used in our ministry today. My wife, the former Betty Smithey, serves alongside me and God has blessed our ministry in a tremendous way. Praise the Lord!

Michael (Tiny) Coghill

"Growing up in Clarksville, I, as a young teen, would drop by the Christian Service Men's Center, early in the morning, after delivering the Nashville newspapers. It was there that I first met Brother Harold, and other stalwart Christians who influenced my life. The next time I met Brother Harold was after I came back from a tour in Vietnam and became a member of the First Christian Church. Dr. Bill Corley was our pastor. Brother Harold had a tremendous influence on Dr. Corley's life and preaching. He caught fire in preaching the Gospel and filled up the pews. Brother Harold's life and witness for Jesus has held us spell bound through the years. Youth Challenge, the Russian ministry, tiles for Jesus, Christian Partners, supporting six orphanages in Russia, a TV station to provide a Christian witness for the area are some of the ministries started by Brother Harold and used for the glory of Jesus. He has contributed to our family, and his encouragement contributed to my military and civil service career. But the greatest contribution from Brother Harold was his witness for the Lord Jesus Christ to me.

LTC James C. Savage lll, US Army Retired
Retired Judge Advocate and US Civil Service Attorney

"Seven years ago, my friend, Al Jaynes, told some interesting stories about a man of God, Harold Witmer. Al, along with other men, shipped a 40 foot container of supplies for my family, along with Bibles and clothing for the people of Jamaica.

While in Nashville, I visited Brother Harold to ask for his help in shipping humanitarian supplies to Jamaica, after a hurricane had hit there. I was very concerned about getting various items and finding a place to store them. The prayers that had been offered on behalf of these needs began to be answered that day in an amazing way. There seemed to be no way in the natural to get these things done. That day I learned that God works through those who are willing and have His heartbeat to reach those who are in need.

First of all, Brother Harold stimulated my faith with his "now" stories and prayer together. He said that if I have a vision from God, then He will get it done in answer to the prayers and needs of the people of Jamaica for Bibles, food and other supplies. He said, "Pray, then watch what God will do."

Brother Harold would provide a storage place for my supplies at the Old Feed Warehouse place, and he would supply pallets of tile for the rebuilding of churches, schools and buildings throughout the island of Jamaica.

As I was leaving Brother Harold's office, he introduced me to Chuck Ryan, a will known businessman. Chuck would help take care of the procuring and shipping of Bibles and other supplies to Jamaica.

May God get the glory! I thank God for Brother Harold and his example of faith in action. "

Ken Snider
M-Div Graduate of Vanderbilt Divinity School
Missionary to Jamaica for 32 years

Contents

Acknowledgments

The writing of this book would not have been possible without the helpful contribution of a number of people. First of all, my wife, Gloria, encouraged and supported me in the writing of this book. She critiqued my writing in a kindly and helpful manner, and did the final editing of the chapters.

My oldest son, Joey, helped to edit the chapters and gave invaluable advice on what to include and exclude.

I borrowed from the writings of the late Dr. Bill Corley. His insights and relevant information added to the life of the book. Hubert White's stories about his trips to Russia gave insight to how the teams operated while in Russia.

Harold's wife, Faye, checked and corrected the manuscript several times. She also shared her journal notes from her trip to East Germany with Brother Harold and the team. Her notes made a great contribution to the writing of two chapters.

Bobby Greenwood's generous sharing of his experiences with Brother Harold inspired the writing of a chapter.

A number of others gave verbal or written contributions to the story. Their sharing helped to give more validity to the book. I owe them and I am grateful for their contributions.

I

Preface

I first met Brother Harold in the early 1960's. At that time, I came to Clarksville to be the Youth for Christ Director. After the Youth for Christ Rallies on Saturday nights, I would join Brother Harold and the staff at the Christian Service Men's Center in witnessing to the soldiers. Also other Saturday nights, I joined Brother Harold to go out on the streets sharing the Gospel with the soldiers, and inviting them to the center for snacks and a place to relax. During that time, I formed a friendship with Brother Harold that has continued through the years. Several years ago, I felt that someone should write Brother Harold's story. At least two people, had written several chapters on Brother Harold's biography, but were not able to finish. Last May, while I was visiting in Clarksville, I felt led of the Lord to commit myself to writing Brother Harold's life story. That commitment came as a conviction, that Brother Harold's life story would be a challenge and a blessing to the Christian Body and a positive witness to the lost. With that in mind, I praise the Lord for the opportunity to write Brother Harold's story. May God take the witness of these words and use them for His honor and glory, and for the advancement of His Kingdom. Amen

Brother Harold's Early Years

Harold's mother looked out the window and saw him and his younger brother on the railroad tracks. "Harold, get off the tracks. For heaven's sake whatta ya doing taking your brother on the tracks? Don't you know a train can come at any time?"

Harold's earliest memories are of living in a small white house near the railroad tracks.

When his mom told his dad about it, he became upset and decided to move the family to another location. They moved to a neighborhood in York, Pennsylvania.

In 1943, when Harold turned seven-years-old, his dad went into the navy. The family cried as they waved goodbye to their dad who boarded the train packed full of soldiers.

Even though Harold was past the age to start school, he had not yet entered elementary school. His mother helped him start in the first grade, but from the beginning, he had a difficult time.

Harold was the oldest of eight children, and even at seven-years-of age, he realized that he needed to be responsible for his siblings.

He was held back in the second grade, because Harold had never learned to read. Perhaps the many tumultuous events in his young life distracted him.

In 1945 his dad came home from the war. He bought a 65-acre farm in Glen Rock, near York. The old log cabin that came with the farm presented a challenge for the family. It had no electricity or water. While Mr.Witmer worked at a plant in York, he spent many hours after work and on the weekends, fixing up the log cabin. Soon the house had electricity and water.

Harold became closer to his dad during this time, as he helped him renovate the log cabin and work on the farm.

Horses, cows, chickens and all other farm animals soon inhabited the farm. One day Harold asked his dad, "Dad, how are we going to farm the land to make crops?"

"Son, we're going to plow with our two horses and the new plow. You're going to have to be the main farmer. You know, I've got to stay with my job in York."

So, Harold, at an early age, ran the Witmer farm. The farm work gave him some rich experiences, but his heavy responsibility of working on the farm caused him to neglect his school work.

One day he asked his dad, "Dad, may I drop out of school? I don't have time for school and the farm."

"Yes, you can, Harold. You know your mom and I never did finish school. We had to go to work early to help support our families, also."

Since Harold did not attend school, he had more time to think up things to do for fun. Harold and his younger brother tried to set up a cowboy movie scene where they had galloping horses pulling a stagecoach. The horses stampeded and raced all about the farm pulling the wagon behind them. When their dad came home from work and heard about the run-away horses, he decided to sell them.

He said, "Spooked horses are a danger to the children."

Harold and his younger brother looked at one another knowing that their movie scenario did not turn out too good.

Later on Mr. Witmer bought a John Deere tractor for the farm. Harold enjoyed driving the tractor. It made his farm work easier. The tractor had a light to use for night driving, and this gave Harold the opportunity to do a lot of work in the evenings.

Brother Harold

Teen-age boys, sooner or later, want a car. Harold was no different. He saved up his money and his dad helped him buy his first automobile. Harold felt it was time for a change in his life. He said to his dad, "Dad, I don't want to spend the rest of my life on the farm. I want to go get a job in York."

"Okay Harold. You've done a good job running the farm, and you can help by working on weekends and after workday each day.

"Where can I get a job, Dad?"

"Mary Shenberger is the manager at the sewing factory. I'll check with her about you working there. She's a nice lady."

The following week Harold went to work on his first job at the sewing factory, delivering cloth to a thousand women. He liked his job and he was able to drive back and forth to work, but there was a stirring in Harold's heart that troubled him.

A New Life in Christ

One night Harold was sitting out on the porch looking up at the stars. Is there a God up there?

A prayer formed in Harold's heart and mind: "God, if Your up there with all those stars and things, then prove it to me."

That same week he went to town with some friends and saw the movie, Mr. Texas, starring Red Harper and Billy Graham. The film touched his heart and deepened his hunger to know God. He knew that he needed to become a Christian, but he didn't know how.

Later on Harold and his friends discussed the movie. "Do you think a person can know God?" Harold questioned them.

"We don't know Harold. We don't think much about such things."

Several nights later Harold drove to town to go skating. He passed the large, white building of the York Gospel Center. Each time he had passed this church he had felt an impression to go in. That night something tugged at his heart.   He decided to stop and attend the church service.

The pastor felt impressed to change his sermon to John the third chapter. He emphasized how Nicodemus came to Jesus because he wanted to know God.   It's obvious that the Holy Spirit guided the pastor, because Harold had also come wanting to know God.

Jesus told Nicodemus that he must be born again. The pastor explained that a person is born again when they turn from their old way of life in sin to commit their life in faith to Jesus, believing that He died for their sins on the cross and rose again from the dead.

Pastor Boyer continued, "Jesus opened the way from heaven to earth and made it possible for us to know God."

He said, "If you know Jesus, you know God, for Jesus came to show us what God is like."

The sermon caught Harold's attention. Here was a man who wanted to know God, and Jesus told him how he could know God. A person must be born again before he can see the Kingdom of God, and the pastor explained how a person could be born again.

During the invitation, nobody came forward…there was no movement. But on the last verse Harold came down the aisle. He wanted Jesus in his life…he wanted to know God.

Brother Charles Shirey met him and counseled with him about his commitment to trust in Jesus as Lord and Savior. After quoting Revelation 3:20: "Behold, I stand at the door and knock, if any man hears My voice and opens the door, I'll come in…," Brother Shirey asked Harold, "Are you ready to open the door of your heart and invite Jesus to come in?"

Harold said, "I'm ready."

Harold prayed a short, heart-felt prayer; "Lord, please forgive my sins. I need You..I want to know You as my Savior and Lord. Please come into my heart."

After praying with Harold, Brother Shirey introduced him to the pastor, Ralph Boyer. Brother Boyer took him to his office where he encouraged him to become active in the church, read God's Word and become an active witness for Christ.

When Harold returned home, his mom asked him, "Harold, did you go to the skating rink?"

"No Mom, I went to church. Tonight, Mom, I prayed to receive Jesus as my Savior and Lord."

"That's great! Your grandmother will be proud of you."

"Mom, I know something wonderful happened to me, because I feel a real peace in my heart."

"Now son don't take religion too serious. You know how your grandmother used to drag us to all those street meetings."

Later when Brother Charles Shirey counseled with Harold, he gave him a Gospel of John. "Harold, I want you to read this Gospel of John. It will tell you many things you need to know as a new believer in Christ."

Harold took the Gospel of John home and tried to read it, but he could not because of his lack of education. He felt frustrated because of his limitations. He prayed, "Lord, I want to know more about You and I want to read Your Word. Help me to learn how to read. Amen"

Harold's prayer was about to be answered in a way that would amaze him.

Brother Charles followed up on Harold and came to the farm to talk with him. Harold had not returned to church, because he felt embarrassed that he could not read.

"Harold, we've missed you at church. Why haven't you come back to church?"

"Well, I've been busy here on the farm."

"Have you read the Gospel of John?"

"No sir, I haven't. There are so many things I've had to do that I just haven't gotten around to it."

"Harold, God's Word is important for you. You can't grow without it. Romans 10:17 says, "Faith comes from hearing and hearing by the Word of God."

The following Sunday Harold came to church and sat with the young people. The pastor asked the young people to stand and read some verses from the Bible. A beautiful young lady, Faye Kreidler, standing next to Harold, noticed that Harold struggled with his reading.

After church Faye said to Harold, "I noticed that you had some trouble trying to read the verses in the Bible. Would you like for me to help you learn how to read better?"

"Yes, I would, Faye. You know, I work on our farm and I had to drop out of school. I really want to learn how to read, so I can read the Bible."

"You come to my house one or two times a week, and I'll be glad to help you with your reading."

Faye began to teach Harold the fundamentals of reading. She broke down the words into syllables and taught him the very basics of learning how to read.

Faye said, "Harold, because you're so motivated, you're going to learn how to read quickly."

"I'm motivated because I want to read God's Word. Before now, I wasn't interested in school or learning, but now it's exciting."

Harold's desire to learn how to read and Faye's desire to help him resulted in a fruitful and enduring relationship.

Harold and Faye

Harold quickly became involved in the Youth Program, and he soon became one of the youth leaders.

Harold was one of the few young people who had a car. He picked up other young people and took them to church with him to participate in youth activities and worship services.

One night after a youth service, Harold asked Faye, "Can I take you and your friend home tonight?"

"Sure, that would be nice."

They took the scenic route home, and on the way, they passed a cemetery that had a well-lit mausoleum.

Harold asked, "What's that?"

Faye answered, "That's a mausoleum. You want to stop and look at it?"

"Sure, I do. I've never seen one."

They approached the well-lighted mausoleum, and Faye opened the door and they went in to the small compartment. She pulled out one of the drawers that had three beautiful urns in it.

Harold asked, "What's in those pretty jars?"

"It's the ashes of people who have died and have been cremated."

"Dead people's ashes? Hey, let's get outta here. This isn't for me."

Faye later recalled that evening. She laughed and said, "Our first date was to a mausoleum. When Harold realized what was in the beautiful urns, he made a quick exit."

It was during this time that Faye used the Gospel of John to continue to teach Harold how to read and write. Harold made progress in reading and increased his knowledge of the Bible; however, he still struggled with his reading.

By the end of the summer, they began to date seriously. The next spring they requested permission from Faye's parents to get married, after she graduated from high school. Their answer was a negative one. They counseled her, "We'll give you permission after your first year in college, but if you wait until you graduate, we'll give our whole-hearted endorsement for your marriage."

Faye's parents, Mr. and Mrs. Kreidler, wisely wanted Faye and Harold to have more time in their decision to get married. They projected the possibility of

Faye finding someone else in college who would be more compatible with her music career.

But the Kreidlers most of all wanted Faye to marry in God's will with God's man for her life. At that point of time, they didn't think it would be Harold.

Witnessing Out of the Overflow

When Harold started taking the commands of Christ seriously, he determined to become a witness for Christ. He went to the City Park in York looking for someone to tell about the Good News. He met a homeless man on a park bench. The man was unshaven and his clothes were torn and unkempt. He reeked of the smell of cheap rum.

After speaking with the man, Harold said, "I want to share some great news with you. Jesus can and will save you from your sins. He died for your sins and He will forgive you. If you trust your life to Him, He will change your life. He saved me and came into my life. Now, I have a real peace."

"Do you really believe that?"

"Yes, I do with all my heart. I don't have any doubts, because Jesus has given me real peace."

The man said, "I think you do believe it, but I don't know whether He can do it for me, or not."

"Yes, He can do the same for you. Once I was empty but Jesus has filled me with a real joy and peace. He'll do the same for you."

"I don't know…"

"You know that big white church over there. That's where I met Jesus. Why don't you come? Jesus will fill the empty place in your life, if you ask Him too."

The man stood up. "I'll…I'll think about it…"

The homeless man decided to go to the church for the next service. When the altar call was given, he came and fell on his knees and prayed to receive Christ into his life.

Harold was ecstatic. He saw the first fruits of his witness for Christ.

One day, Faye asked Harold, "Would you like to give your testimony on the radio? I have an hour program, and I think it would be good for you to share how you came to know the Lord."

"Sure, Faye, I'll be glad to do it."

At Harold's work place, the sewing factory, he shared with his friends that he had come to know Jesus and his life had changed. Some of his old friends didn't believe it at first, but as time went by, they saw a new

15

Harold who didn't curse or tell dirty jokes. They also recognized a new dimension in Harold's life.

Mary Shenberger, the manager, came by Harold's work station, and he shared with her how he had trusted Jesus. She took his hand and congratulated him on his new life and told him that she would pray for him.

Harold's profession of faith in Jesus, and his new life, impacted the employees at South Pine Night Ware. There was a campaign started to stop using profanity. Many of the women expressed a desire to see their husbands saved.

When Mary Shenberger, dropped by Harold's work station one day, he told her," I'm going to be on the radio and give my testimony of how I met Jesus."

"That's wonderful, Harold. I saw you yesterday sharing your testimony with some of the men. Your face was shining."

Harold looked surprised. "It was?"

"Yes, you were beaming from the joy you have in Jesus. Harold, I want you to share your testimony with my staff. Would you do that?"

"Yes, Mrs. Shenberger, I'll be happy anytime to tell others what Jesus has done for me. Thank you for supporting and encouraging me as a Christian."

From the early days of his Christian life, Harold felt an inner compulsion to share Jesus, the giver of eternal life, with others. This desire to witness to the saving power of Jesus continued on through Harold's life in the army.

A Soldier for Jesus and Uncle Sam

After Faye left York to study at Northwestern Conservatory of Music, Harold felt lonely and restless. He wanted to leave York and see and do new things.

Harold's friend, Donald, told him that the Army provided a way to serve his country and to also get an education; so, Harold decided to join the army Harold joined the Army.

He did his basic training at Fort Dix in New Jersey. The rigorous training stretched every muscle in Harold's body and challenged every brain cell in his head. The drill sergeants drove the new recruits from morning to night. Harold never dreamed that the army would be this tough.

At night, when Harold fell into his rack, he cried out to the Lord to give him strength to make it through basic training. The Lord answered Harold's prayers, and he came through this challenging period.

After eight weeks of basic training at Dix, he got a fifteen-day leave. This break gave him time to regroup and renew his spirit.

A Soldier for Jesus and Uncle Sam

Harold was assigned to Ft. Campbell. It was there that he enrolled in Jump School. If Harold thought basic training was rough, Jump School took rough up another notch. Airborne training challenged every fiber in Harold's body.

When Harold got his first weekend pass, he went to Clarksville. While there, he ran into Johnny Shearer, a young man he had met at Fort Dix. Harold had led Johnny to trust Jesus as Lord and Savior at Fort Dix. They had a joyful reunion.

Later on that evening, they heard about a program called the "G.I. Gospel Hour." The program was at the chapel of the First Baptist Church. Chief Petty Officer James Varian from the Clarksville Naval Base was the main speaker.

James Varian challenged his listeners to commit themselves to the Lordship of Jesus Christ. When the invitation was given, Harold went forward committing himself to follow Jesus with all his heart.

Harold's friend, Johnny Shearer, came right behind him. He said, "I don't know what you're coming forward for, but if it's what you need to do, then I need to do it too."

James Varian counseled with Harold and Johnny. He said, "Jesus is the victory. Keep Him before you, men."

Varian gave them his address and said, "If you need help or anything, come over at any time."

The next week, Johnny Shearer finished Jump School and left for Germany. Harold had not finished his training. He had jumped from the twenty-five foot tower twenty-six times, but he did not get his jumps right enough to please the instructors.

After this Harold transferred to the 11th Artillery that the airborne called a "leg unit."

The letters sent by Faye encouraged Harold to keep walking with Jesus. She usually returned his letters with corrections. This became his daily reading and writing lesson.

During these difficult times, Harold often went to visit Jim and Dixie Varian in Clarksville. They took him in like a son and counseled him in the Word of God.

It was during this time that Harold grew in the grace of the Lord, but God sent someone else into his life to further grow him in his faith.

An Extraordinary Platform for Witness

One day Harold had the opportunity to preach at the Post Stockade. He preached on Jesus' message to Nicodemus, "You must be born again." When he gave the invitation, a large number of soldiers came forward.

Colonel Cecil Hill, a full bird colonel, stood in the back listening and giving attention to the response to the message. After the service, Colonel Hill approached Harold. "Soldier, I want you to come by my office tomorrow."

The following day, Colonel Hill wasted no time in getting to the purpose of Harold's visit to his office. "Private Witmer, I want you to work in my office. I'll take care of every thing concerning your present outfit. You can start tomorrow."

The colonel was in charge of the Post finances and all the accountants on the Post worked for him. He was the highest-ranking colonel on the Post, in his grade.

Harold started to work in the office as a file clerk, making plates and cards on soldiers coming from overseas. The office didn't realize that Harold still struggled to read and write until he had messed up the entire filing section of the Post Finance Office.

The major in charge of the office called Harold into his office. "Private Witmer, you've screwed up our entire filing system. I don't want you around here anymore. You're fired!"

After going for a week without a job, Harold was called back in by the major. The major realized that if word got back to Colonel Hill that Harold had been fired, he might be in trouble.

The major still did not know that Harold struggled with reading and writing. They put him to work on what they called, "commercial accounts." After several weeks in this new work, Harold messed up this section, also. The major had had it. "Private Witmer, you're outta here. You're fired!"

This time Harold was without a job for two months. He became a man of leisure who got paid for doing nothing. He passed the time by strolling about the Post. He spent some time at the Base Chapel talking with the Chaplain's Assistant. At other times, he met old buddies at the PX.

An Exraordinary Platform for Witness

One day Harold met Jim Harrier and they quickly became friends. Jim was an Airborne Trooper. While he was home on furlough, he had wandered into a church and got saved. He and Harold were excited because they had had similar experiences. They talked all evening about Jesus and how He had changed their lives.

When Jim came back from leave, he shared with some of his buddies about his experience of salvation, but they mocked him. He realized that living for Jesus called for an all out commitment, so he slipped back into his old lifestyle.

It was during this time that the Lord led Harold into his life. He encouraged Jim in the Lord and helped get him back on track.

One day Harold told Jim about the Christian colonel on the Post. He said, "The colonel really helps me understand the Bible. How'd you like to meet him?"

Jim looked at Harold with disbelief. "Meet a colonel? Are you kidding? Privates don't go around meeting colonels."

"This colonel is different. "

"Harold, I believe you're putting me on. I won't believe it 'til I see it."

"Well, I'm gonna visit the colonel this evening. You wanna go with me?"

"Yeah, I gotta see this."

When Harold and Jim approached the colonel's house, Jim could see the colonel's name on the door. However, when Harold knocked on the door, Jim jumped off the porch and hid behind the hedge bushes near the door.

The colonel came to the door. "Well, Harold. Come in."

"Colonel I want you to meet my friend, Jim Harrier. He's a…"

When he turned to introduce Jim, he wasn't there. He was still behind the bushes."

Harold called, "Jim, where are ya?"

Jim stepped out from behind the bushes. "I'm coming."

Although he was scared to death, Jim went into the colonel's house. During that first visit, he wasn't able to relax. He sat stiff as a poker and said, "Yes sir, or no sir."

He would stand at attention every time he stood up.

An Exraordinary Platform for Witness

The Colonel asked Jim, "Would you like to work for me?"

"Yes sir."

"I need a draftsman in my office. Do you have any experience in that line of work?"

"Yes sir, I've worked as a commercial artist."

"You're hired. You report to my office next Monday. I'll take care of matters with your unit."

The Colonel asked, "Harold, how's your work coming along in the office?"

"Colonel, I'm not working now. They fired me."

"They fired you? I'll talk to the major about that."

The next day the Colonel called the major into his office. He said to the Major, "I don't understand how you could fire a man like Private Witmer. He's a valuable man to have around."

The Major said with disbelief, "Yes sir, Colonel."

"Well major, from now on Private Witmer's going to go to work for me."

The Colonel gave Harold a job in his own office. He became the colonel's personal driver, clerk, runner and right-hand man.

Harold spoke about his time with the colonel. "Anything he wanted, I was Johnny-on-the-spot. I really enjoyed my work. I could ask the colonel Bible questions that came to my mind. Whenever I drove up to the gate in the colonel's car, the guards always saluted, whether the colonel was in the car, or not. When I drove up to an office to get something for the Colonel, everyone snapped to attention and quickly got what I came for. I was soon known on the Post as the 'little colonel'.

Harold and Jim often went into the colonel's office and had Bible study with him. They sometimes went into his office to ask him questions concerning some subject in the Bible that they had discussed together.

The others in the office were amazed that Harold and Jim would just willy-nilly go into the colonel's office to talk with him. They didn't understand what was going on. The Chief Clerk, a Master Sergeant, who was new in the office, especially took notice to the two privates going into the colonel's office without special permission to do so.

The sergeant chewed them out and said that they must have permission to go into the colonel's office. After that, Harold and Jim did not go into the colonel's office as often as before, knowing that it upset the sergeant.

One day the Colonel asked Harold and Jim, "Why aren't you coming into my office for study and questions like you did before? Is there a problem?"

Harold said, "Colonel, the Chief Clerk gets upset when he sees us going into your office without getting special permission from him. We don't want to cause any trouble."

"Well, I'll see about that. I'll talk to the sergeant. You all can come into my office anytime you want too. You work for me, not the sergeant."

The Colonel called the sergeant into his office and had a talk with him. When he came out, he was shaking his head in disbelief. He said to Harold and Jim: "I don't believe it. How can two privates be so close to a colonel? In all my years in the army, I've never seen anything like it. What's this man's army coming too?"

Harold had a great platform for witness in the army, but the Lord gave him even a greater platform to share Christ.

Expanding a Witness

During this time, the Colonel also worked with the Christian Businessmen's Organization. CBO is a world-wide organization composed of Christian businessmen, from different churches, who come together for fellowship, worship and ministry. Their main purpose is to win other businessmen to faith in Christ.

The Colonel was often called upon to be their main speaker. He began to take Harold and Jim with him, when he spoke in cities all over the Southeast.

Since Harold did some work in the colonel's office as a file clerk, the colonel found out that Harold could hardly read or write. He sent him down to the Education Center to be tested. He tested on a third grade level. They advised Harold to start with third grade workbooks.

Harold told of the struggle he had to learn how to read: "I took my third grade work books down to my company and studied them right there. Some of the guys laughed and made fun of me, but I didn't have a choice. I wanted to go back to school and to get an education, so I had to start at the beginning. It was hard, but I did it."

Expanding a Witness

Harold passed on to the fourth and then the fifth grade. Eventually, he was able to read and write. He wrote Faye two or three letters a week and she always helped him by returning every one of his letters with the misspelled words corrected.

While visiting in the cities that had Christian Businessmen's Organizations, Harold and Colonel Hill also visited a number of Christian Service Men's Centers.

One day the Colonel, Harold, Jim and several other men in the Clarksville area, felt God leading them to start a center in the downtown Clarksville area to reach out to soldiers who came to town on a pass.

They began to pray for two specific things. First, they prayed for the right person to direct the center, and secondly, they prayed for a building to house the activities of the center. While looking for a building, they heard that the Conroy brothers, John and Paul, had just bought a large cavernous building in the downtown area of Clarksville. The brothers didn't know what they were going to do with it.

The men talked to John and Paul about renting the building to be used for a Christian Servicemen's Center, and they both agreed to rent the entire second floor to them. God answered the prayers of the board members.

The next step was to find someone to direct the activities of the center. Colonel Hill retired to work at a civil job. Jim Harrier enrolled at Austin Peay State University and Jim Varian received orders for duty in California. At this same time, Harold received his honorable discharge from the army.

The board members for the Christian Servicemen's center felt led to call Harold as the Director of the Center. His duties would consist of organizing activities for the soldiers who dropped by the center, enlisting volunteer personnel to share the Gospel, enlisting church groups to help with food and entertainment and to raise money to support the ongoing work of the center.

Like Moses, Harold felt inadequate for the task, but he felt that if God placed him in that position, then God would provide all that he needed. And he was right on!

Even though Harold and Faye had gone their separate ways after her graduation from high school, they kept their love growing for one another through their letters.

Expanding a Witness

Faye had received a scholarship from North-western Conservatory of Music in Minneapolis. Faye's parents felt that after one year at the Conservatory she would find someone else in her field.

After Faye left for college, Harold enlisted in the army. He wanted to go to Bible School, but they rejected him because he did not have a high school diploma. A friend told him that he could get his G.E.D. in the military.

While in the military, Harold and Faye exchanged two or three letters a week. She diligently corrected all of Harold's letters and returned them in her letters. Through this correspondence, Harold continued to improve in his reading and writing.

Faye graduated Magna Cum Laude in three years from the Northwestern Conservatory of Music; about the same time, Harold received his honorable discharge from the army. The Board Members of the Christian Servicemen's Center asked Harold to become the Director of the Center.

When Harold proposed to Faye in one of his letters, she said "Yes" to his proposal. They set the date for the wedding for the last of August.

A number of people did not think Faye and Harold were a good fit for marriage, because they came from different backgrounds. In speaking to this, Harold said: "A lot of people could not see us together. I had been poorly educated and Faye was a college honor graduate. But there was no doubt in our minds, because we felt that God had put us together."

After her graduation in August, Faye came to Fort Campbell. She and Harold were married at Chapel #9 on the Post. The reception was held at the Christian Servicemen's Center.

After their honeymoon, Harold and Faye returned to Clarksville to direct the Center. God was going to use this newly married couple in a mighty way to touch hundreds of soldiers with the Gospel of Jesus Christ.

A Light House for the Lost

The Christian Servicemen's Center opened in June 1958, for the purpose of sharing the Gospel with servicemen and to provide recreation and fellowship for them. Everyone was welcome. Young men and women could come in off the street and receive free food, a place to lounge, read magazines and to listen to records.

The Christian workers in the center would present to them a simple plan of salvation and point them to Jesus Christ, as Savior.

Harold and Faye lived in an apartment on the second floor of the center. They coordinated the activities of the center, along with their own participation in witnessing and counseling those who came in to visit.

One of the many blessings that resulted in the center being made available to be used for ministry to the servicemen was the renting of the center from John and Paul Conroy. They agreed to rent the center for seventy-five dollars a month, but sometimes Harold was unable pay the rent. At those times, the Conroy's donated it. When Harold had the money, he always paid them.

Paul and John Conroy never complained or pushed for the rent. They were thankful that the center was meeting the needs of many servicemen. What makes this even more of a blessing/miracle from the Lord is that the Conroy's also would furnish the cost of the utilities to go with the building.

The building that housed the center is a block long and a half block wide. To furnish air conditioning in the summer and heating in the winter really involved a generous sacrifice on the part of the Conroy's.

Many church groups and individuals brought food and drinks to the center.

When they needed food, or other materials, Harold said, "God will provide."

And God did provide for their needs. Harold believed that God would care and provide for them. He claimed the promise in Philippines 4:19, "And my God will supply all your needs according to His riches in glory in Christ Jesus."

With all the blessings of seeing God work at the center, the Lord blessed Harold and Faye with two sons, Timothy and Steven.

A Light House for the Lost

When Faye came home from the hospital after giving birth to Steven, Eunice Pelonero helped settle her in her home. Eunice said, "Faye, I'm going to cook the evening meal, okay?"

"Thanks Eunice. I hope you can find some food in the pantry."

Eunice didn't find anything in the pantry. Eunice called some of the military friends of the center and explained the situation to them. Captain and Mrs. Harvey Hartman soon arrived with a large box of food. Later on, others came by bringing food. They had more than enough food for everyone.

Faye remembered that happening, and said, "From that time on, we never wanted for food."

The Christian Servicemen's Center touched many lost soldiers and led them to know Christ Jesus and the forgiveness of their sins. The strong Christian witness of the center also spoke to the lives of many soldiers who were out of fellowship with the Lord.

Jim Marlow grew up in a small town in Florida. While in high school, he made a profession of faith in Christ. After joining the army, he began to drift away from the Lord. While he was stationed at Ft. Campbell, he heard about the Christian Servicemen's Center.

Jim told about his first experience in the center: "When I came into the center, I met Harold Witmer and Jim Harrier and all the other men there. I was amazed at how these men took a stand for Christ and made it a priority to do personal witnessing. I realized how far short I had fallen in the eyes of the Savior. I got on my knees with Harold and asked the Lord to forgive me."

When Jim finished his tour in the army, he went on to Southeastern Bible College in Birmingham, Alabama.

After Sgt. Lindy Lopez experienced salvation at a small church in Virginia, he came to Ft. Campbell. The Christian Servicemen's center provided Sgt. Lopez a place to connect with other Christians and a place to serve the Lord.

Sgt. Lopez said, "After my transfer to Ft. Campbell, I found real Christian fellowship at the Clarksville Servicemen's Center. Not only did the center offer a place for me to grow but also a place to serve. While serving, I grew in my own spiritual life. God also blessed me in many other ways. I give God the glory!"

A Light House for the Lost

When the Christian Servicemen's Center closed at ten each evening, there were usually a number of soldiers still in the center. Before closing, Harold gathered all those present into a prayer circle. Sometimes there would be as many as twenty or more in the circle. Each person was given the opportunity to pray.

Harold said, "Often, when we had the prayer circle, there was one or two lost soldiers in the circle. We never prayed around the circle without the lost men in that circle professing Christ as Lord and Savior. Those prayer circles were powerful."

With the growth of the Witmer family, Harold and Faye moved to a house in Clarksville, but someone needed to be at the center at all times. The Lord provided that someone.

When Harold led a Bible study at Ft. Campbell, Glen Davis attended the study. Glen impressed Harold with his openness to the Gospel and his eagerness to follow Jesus as a disciple.

One weekend Glen came to the center. He said to Harold, "I wish I could witness to others like you. I'd give anything to lead one person to Christ."

"Glen, if you stay on your knees and ask God to give you a love for people, I promise you that you'll be able to lead someone to Christ."

Glen went back to one of the prayer rooms in the back of the building and spent several hours on his knees. When he came out, God did something exciting to encourage Glen's faith, as He often does with His children. A soldier had come into the center and had picked up some Gospel tracts. After reading a few tracts, he went straight to Glen and said, "How do I go about meeting God?"

Glen looked around for Harold, but Harold, aware of what was going on, kept out of sight. Glen had no choice. He now had the opportunity to lead someone to know Christ as Savior, and there was no one else to do it. He did help that young man come to know Jesus as Savior and Lord. He was ecstatic about bringing him to Jesus.

From that day on, Glen became a dynamic witness for Christ. Later on he moved into the center. Glen and his wife, Jeannie, led scores of young men to experience Christ and influenced many others in their Christian walk.

A Light House for the Lost

But Brother Harold was moving on to another job. He was about to have one of the great experiences of his life. At the beginning of his new job, he never dreamed of the extent of how God was going to use him in a "hands on, rubber meet the road" experience. Revival was just around the corner.

Revival at the Trane Plant

Since The Christian Servicemen' Center was not a full time job, Harold got a job at the Trane Plant, a plant which manufactures air conditioners.

Harold determined to live for Jesus at the plant. The Trane Plant's moral and spiritual atmosphere resembled that of the army. When the men came together, they forgot their moral values. Their language became obscene and their jokes dirty.

Harold's work at the plant was to operate a shear using a blueprint to cut the metal to the right size, and then pass it on down the assembly line to be processed for a particular use.

The first two years at the plant, were the most difficult for Harold. Although he tried to be a witness for Christ, the men around him were not interested. Many times Harold came home from work and said to Faye, "Tomorrow is my last day at work," but Harold didn't quit.

The Lord gave Harold the strength and endurance to hold on during that difficult time. The Heavenly

Father had wonderful plans for Harold at the Trane Plant, but he didn't realize it at that time. A revival was about to break out at the plant.

One of the men who worked with Harold at the plant was Bobby Ladd. Bobby, a rugged individual, used crude language. Since he worked beside Harold, he had to listen to Bobby day after day. Bobby's incessant chatter grated on Harold's nerves.

One day when Harold worked on the second shift, he got off at 11pm. Since Bobby got off at the same time, Harold asked him, "Bobby, would you mind driving me home?"

"Sure Harold, no problem."

On the way home, they stopped at a café for a cup of coffee. While sitting and enjoying their coffee, a drunken man came in and began cursing. Amid the curses, he quoted Scripture verses

After they left the café, they pulled up into Harold's driveway. Bobby turned off the engine. He wanted to talk. "Did that drunk know what he was talking about? You know- about the Bible verses."

"I don't know if he knew what he was talking about, but he quoted the verses perfectly."

"Harold, would you mind explaining those verses to me?"

From midnight until 2pm, Harold explained the verses to Bobby.

At 2pm Harold said, "Bobby I'm tired and need to get some sleep, but if you're interested, I'll talk to you all night."

"Harold, do you think I would talk to you until two in the morning, if I wasn't interested?"

"Bobby, do you mean that you're interested enough to give your life to Christ?"

"Yes, I am. This is what I want for my life."

Harold said, "Bobby, I'm going to pray for you and when I finish, I want you to pray and ask Jesus to forgive you of all your sins and invite Him to come into your heart. If you ask Him to come into your heart, He will come into your life."

After Harold prayed, Bobby prayed with tears coursing down his cheeks. "Lord Jesus, forgive me for all my sins, I'm sorry for my sins and for the sorry life that I've lived. Come into my life, Lord Jesus and be the Lord of my life."

Revival at the Trane Plant

From what happened in Bobby's life later on, it is clear that at that moment of prayer, Bobby Ladd was transformed, born again by the Spirit of God.

The next day, Harold decided not to mention Bobby's commitment to anyone at the work place. Bobby was on his own, and Harold watched to see what he was going to do and say about his profession of faith.

Bobby shared with each one of his friends that Jesus had come into his life and he was a new person. His friends said, "Bobby, talk is cheap. We'll watch and see what kind of life you'll live now."

Brother Harold was thrilled as he watched Bobby share with his friends. Bobby immediately became concerned for his other friends. He brought Frankie Farrell to Harold and asked him to show Frankie the same verses that he had shown him. That night after work, Frankie came by Brother Harold's house and Brother Harold led him to open his heart to receive Christ Jesus as Savior and Lord. A revival started!

Bobby and Frankie took a stand for Christ amid their co-workers at the Plant. As a result many others came to salvation in Christ and other fellow Christians began to come out and identify themselves as Believers in Christ.

George Graves was another one of those who began sharing his faith with others. He started sharing with his friend, Jim Yeatts. Jim's background was similar to that of Bobby Ladd's background. He was hard and tough and talked loud and rough. He had laughed in George's face many times, as George tried to share Jesus with him.

Jim also managed a service station that he moonlighted on the side. One night, when he was alone at the station, he felt the burden and weight of sin and fell on his knees to ask the Lord Jesus to save him. When he got off his knees, he was a new man in Christ.

Jim Yeatts, who was a loud mouth for the devil, became a loud mouth for Jesus Christ. He became the most vocal witness in the Trane Plant. The word began spreading throughout the Trane Plant that something new and exciting was happening in the lives of many people. As the word spread in the Trane Plant, so did the Word of God.

Christians at the Trane Plant began to study the Word of God and witness. Many workers came to know the living Savior, Jesus Christ. Revival came to the Trane Plant!

When Christians are revived, it opens their eyes to see the spiritual needs around them. The Trane Plant revival opened the eyes of Jim Yeatts and Brother Harold Witmer to see the needs of the youth of Clarksville.

The Birth of Youth Challenge

The revival at the Trane Plant resulted in the birth of Youth Challenge. After Jim Yeatts came to experience Jesus in his life, he began to see the needs around him. He not only saw the needs at the plant, but he began to see the needs of a lost world. It started as he looked at Clarksville.

One day Jim Yeatts brought to Brother Harold's attention several articles in the newspaper about teenage crime in Clarksville. He said, "Brother Harold, we need to do something about this. These young people need a youth center. If the young people had a place to go, they wouldn't get in trouble. Brother Harold, you need to open a youth center."

Brother Harold said, "This is the city's problem and not ours. Why should we get involved in this?"

Jim Yeatts did not give up on the youth problem. Every day he told Brother Harold that somebody needed to do something with the young people in Clarksville. He said, "Brother Harold, somebody needs to care for these young people. Many of them are only thirteen years of age and are already getting in trouble with the police."

Brother Harold said, "Jim, I don't know anything about working with young people. I wouldn't know the first thing of how to start."

Jim Yeatts wouldn't give up about the needs of the young people. He asked, "Brother Harold, would you start praying with me about the needs of the youth?"

"Sure Jim, when we get off work, we can sit in your car and have prayer before we go home."

After a week of praying with Jim, the Lord also laid a burden on Brother Harold's heart for the young people of Clarksville. He realized that something needed to be done and somebody needed to take up the responsibility. Brother Harold prayed, "Here, I am Lord, send me."

One evening as Brother Harold and Jim drove up to an old building in New Providence, they saw that it was available to rent for $100.00 a month. They estimated that it would take $2,000.00 in repairs before it could be used.

Brother Harold said, "Jim, I'll give fifty dollars on the first month's rent."

"I've got the other fifty covered. We're in business, Brother Harold."

They had to haul away six loads of trash before they could move into the basement. The building was a total mess. They needed to install two bathrooms and a kitchen. They were working ten hours a day at the plant and, after they got off work, they worked a number of hours at the center.

Brother Harold told Jim, "We can't keep this up. It's gonna break our health."

"God gives extra strength and energy to those who are carrying out His will. Harold, God loves those boys and girls, and He wants to love them through us," Jim said.

While Brother Harold and Jim were working on the building, friends and strangers drove by and asked, "What are you doing?"

Even though Brother Harold and Jim were not quite sure where and how all was going to turn out, they shared their vision: "We're building a center where young people can get off the street and come for entertainment and recreation. While they're here, we'll share with them that God loves them in Jesus."

The Birth of Youth Challenge

Brother Harold and Jim continued to work and little by little the funds, to meet the needs of the center, began to come in. In one prayer service at the center, they prayed for the two bathrooms that needed to be installed. At the end of the service, a man stood up and said, "I'll furnish all the materials needed for the bathrooms."

They needed a certified plumber to install the bathrooms. One day as Harold, Jim and others were painting the center; a plumber walked in and asked them what they were doing. They said, "We're painting this youth center."

"What's a youth center?" The plumber asked.

"A youth center is a place where youth can come for recreation and hear about God's love. We need to put in two bathrooms and also a kitchen for the center."

The plumber got out a tablet and pencil and figured out the cost to install the bathrooms and kitchen and handed it to Harold.

Harold said, "We don't have a dime to give you. If you want to do it, God will repay you."

The plumber turned and walked away.

The next day, another plumber came by the center and volunteered to install the bathrooms free of charge.

That's the way the center operated. The Lord provided what they needed, when they needed it.

While they were remodeling the building, many teenagers came in to ask questions. Harold and Jim used the opportunity to point them to Christ as Savior and Lord. In the first six months of operation, 56 teens made professions of faith in Christ. These young people came from all walks of life. Their witness began to spread over the city.

The facilities for drawing young people to the center were simple. There were two ping-pong tables, a coke machine, a snack bar and a broken down pool table. There was also an office for counseling.

The teens liked the Youth Challenge Center in New Providence, because they considered it their center. It was a place where they were considered important people, loved by God.

Stanley Gower, a reporter from The Clarksville Leaf Chronicle, interviewed Harold about the work of the Youth Challenge Center. He wrote about Harold's earlier life, his conversion and how he came to Clarksville.

The reporter also gave Jim Yeatt's testimony of how God worked in his life and led Jim to work with the youth of Clarksville. When Jim became the manager of the center, he devoted himself to seeing that every young person be given another chance in life.

The newspaper article sparked a response from many people in the area. The telephone started ringing, people came by to ask how they could help and numbers of people also wanted to give financially to the program.

Soon the center was bursting at the seams. Later when Harold spoke to the press about the success of the program, he said, "In general, the boys attitudes have improved, some dropouts have returned to school and many are living more useful lives."

Young people came from all parts of the city to see what was taking place at the center. The center became so crowded that Harold and the staff began to pray for a larger facility.

It did not surprise the staff to see how soon God answered their prayers. They had witnessed many times before how the Lord provided for them in timely fashion.

The Cumberland Drive Baptist Church moved out of their old building into a new one. The church offered the use of their old building to The Youth Challenge Center, until it was sold. This was God's gift to the Youth

Challenge Center, because they did not have a dime to pay for renting a facility.

At this time, Harold felt strongly that he should quit his job at the Trane Plant and devote himself full time to the youth ministry. This was not an easy decision. Faye asked Harold, "Where will our support come from? How are we going to make it?"

Faye's questions were those that any mother with three small children would ask her husband. However, she trusted the Lord's leadership in Harold's life and rested in God's leadership.

Harold's friends at the Trane Plant asked him, "What are you going to do for money?"

Harold replied, "I don't know, but I do know that God wants me to quit my job and go full time. He's leading me to make this move, and He will provide."

Harold quit his job and it was amazing how God provided all the needs of his family's and the center. Money came just when it was needed and it often came from unexpected sources.

Brother Harold, like so many Christians before him, would be tested many more times in the coming days.

Dr. Bill Corley

Who had the most influence on Harold's life, besides his wife Faye? Numbers of people come to mind: Bill Gothard, Bobby Greenwood, Dr. John Laida, Colonel Cecil Hill, Mel Johnson and the list could go on and on; however, Dr. Bill Corley had as much influence, if not more, than all the above mentioned names.

The relationship between Dr. Bill Corley and Harold was based on the common love they had for Jesus, for they came from contrasting backgrounds. Harold grew up in a blue-collar neighborhood where church was not on the family's agenda. He dropped out of school early in life.

On the other hand, Dr. Corley grew up in a middle-class home where church and education was part of the family's tradition. He graduated from college and went on to earn a Master of Divinity and two Doctor of Philosophy degrees.

Harold and Dr. Corley's relationship began when Harold went into his office at the church where Dr. Corley pastored the First Christian Church in Clarksville. Harold had met Brother Bill on another occasion, at a civic club. He asked him, "Brother Bill, would you like to come out to the Youth Challenge Center sometimes and share with our young people how to be saved, you know, how to be born again."

"How to be born again, Harold? What's that?"

Brother Bill had to be impressed by Harold's transparent candor. He didn't dress up his presentation with a lot of words. "Born again, Brother Bill? It means to repent of all your sins and ask Jesus to come and live in your life. When you do that, Jesus comes into your life, just as He promised. Have you done that Brother Bill?"

"Have I done that? I don't know. This born again thing is something I haven't thought about. Where is that in the Bible?"

"Here it is, Brother Bill, John 3:3. I'll read it. See, Jesus said everyone must be born again before they can go to heaven. Have you been born again, Brother Bill?"

"It's strange you ask me something like that, Brother Harold. I've spent years in the ministry and have three theological degrees. Yet, I've never thought about this "born again" business. Doggone it, I need to do something about it. Harold, can you help me experience being 'born again?'"

"I sure can, Brother Bill."

Brother Bill and Brother Harold knelt on the floor and prayed. As Brother Bill prayed tears came rolling down his cheeks. He confessed his sins and asked the living Savior to come into his life. He came off his knees shouting praises to the Lord.

That day, in Dr. Bill Corley's office, the great transformation took place. Brother Bill would never be the same. His preaching, his relationships to others, his outlook on life and his daily life habits changed forever.

Brother Bill's sermons took on a new dimension, a new fire. Some people in the congregation became critical of the pastor's new brand of preaching. Others were fired up by his enthusiastic presentations of the Gospel.

Brother Bill became restless in his position as Pastor of the First Christian Church. He had a vision of reaching out to all people, regardless of their social and economic position, or their race. He soon surrounded himself with men who had a similar vision, including Harold Witmer.

Brother Bill resigned as Pastor of the First Christian Church. He, and forty others, organized the Community Church. Brother Bill became the Pastor of the newly formed congregation. He served as Pastor until his death, thirty years later.

Dr. Bill Corley was, not only a theologian and forceful preacher, he was a patriot. He served as Chief of the Chaplains of the Tennessee State Guard. Shortly before his death, he was commissioned a Brigadier General.

Dr. Corley also served on numerous boards, including university boards.

Another Test of Faith

The Lord had provided larger facilities for the growing Youth Challenge Center, but their faith was soon to be tested again. They were only promised that they could use the building until it was sold, and it could be sold at any time.

If the building was sold, then they had no place to go. Once again, Harold, Jim Yeatts and the group began to pray and ask the Lord, 'What would You have us do?"

One day while Harold was working at the center, a stranger came in. His name was Bob Davis. Harold had never met him and knew nothing about him. Bob Davis said, "I want to help out with the young people. What can I do?"

Harold said, "Great, take this wrecking bar and hammer and help me tear out this old Sunday School room. We're going to make a recreation room that will have ping-pong tables, shuffle boards and other equipment.

While working, Bob asked, "Are you renting this building?"

"No, we're using it free of charge, but it may be sold at any time. If it does sell, we don't have any other place to go."

"Why don't you buy it?"

"We would," Harold said, "but we don't have any money. We depend upon the Lord for everything. If He wants us to have it, then He will provide the money."

A short time later Bob Davis wrote out a check for $7,500.00 for the buying of the building. That was an answer to their prayers and a big step that helped them purchase the building. They moved into their own property.

Two years passed by and more than one hundred young people made commitments to follow Christ through the ministry of the Youth Challenge Center. Bible Clubs were started in high schools and middle schools throughout the city and county. Many young people trusted the Lord through the witness of these Bible Clubs.

A number of young people committed their lives to full time Christian service. Harold often organized trips to visit Bible colleges in the Southeast. They visited campuses in Alabama, South Carolina and Tennessee.

Another Test of Faith

Harold sent letters to Bible colleges asking for students to come and work with the young people for the summer. He only promised them a bed and food. Four students came to work with the Youth Challenge Center during the summer.

These four students were instrumental in starting a camp for the youth. Jim Holleman, owner of a real estate company in Clarksville, offered the use of his farm for the youth camp.

During this time, Frank Gill, a missionary to Mexico, met Harold in Clarksville. Frank and his family were forced to return to the States because of his bad health. Frank lived in Allensville, Kentucky, but he was interested in starting youth work in Clarksville.

A friend in Nashville told Frank, "Before you try to start something in Clarksville, check with Harold Witmer. He has an exciting youth work going on there."

Frank did come and meet Harold and they became good friends. Harold said of Frank, "He's one of the most devoted Christians that I've ever met."

Harold and Frank spent time together praying for the young people and for God's leadership in their lives. Their prayers led to the conviction that they should open a youth camp in Frank's hometown, Allensville. A schoolhouse became available near Frank's home.

They prayed about the schoolhouse and what the Lord wanted them to do with it. The man who owned the property told them they could use it free of charge and could fix it up any way they wanted to renovate it.

Funds came in to launch the new camp. God provided as He always does. Frank also set up a Youth Center in Allensville. God blessed his ministry that received inspiration from Harold's Youth Challenge Center in Clarksville.

Charlie Winchester first met Brother Harold Witmer in Judge Hickerson's courtroom. Charlie had resigned himself to the fact that he was going to the reformatory. Judge Hickerson asked Brother Harold and Rev. Jesse Webb if they would consider taking Charlie into their custody. They took Charlie and Brother Harold began to share with him about trusting Jesus.

Charlie Winchester said, "Harold finally led me to the Lord. When Christ found a dwelling place in my heart, everything became clear."

Today, Charlie Winchester is a member of the Community Church, located across from Gate One at Ft.

Campbell. Charlie finished high school and proudly served in the US Army.

Mike Alexander grew up in Oregon. By the time he turned fifteen, he had already had several brushes with the law and had spent a year in the reformatory. One night, Mike wandered into a church and heard the Good News that Jesus is the Giver of real life, even life eternal. He trusted Jesus to save him.

After several years, Mike enrolled at Southeastern Bible College in Birmingham, Alabama. Mike heard, one day, that a man from Clarksville, Tennessee had come to the campus to recruit summer workers for his youth program.

Mike joined several students in the cafeteria to talk with Harold. Harold described the work and Youth Challenge Center's program. Mike had not interest in the program, for he planned on working with the Navigators for the summer.

Mike described what happened to him in the next week: "The Lord kept speaking to me until school was out. I woke up one morning in Clarksville, and did Harold ever have a motley group of youth. There were some real losers, and I don't mind telling you that I was discouraged. They fought like cats and dogs, robbed the coke machine and came after one another with pool sticks."

Mike finished the summer in Clarksville and came back the following summer to work at the Youth Challenge Center. Thirteen of the young people associated with the center went into full time Christian work. Two of them enrolled at the Southeastern Bible College where Mike attended school.

Who would have thought that in three years time, since the day Mike came to work with the youth in Clarksville, that many of the young people from the center would be traveling hundreds of miles around the Southeast to speak in the name of the Lord Jesus Christ before churches, civic clubs and high schools.

Thousands of young people would come to know Christ through their witness.

All of this happened because Harold Witmer and Jim Yeatts "were not disobedient to the heavenly vision." They visualized what God wanted to do with them, in His hands, to reach the young people of Clarksville.

But God also wanted to teach them to trust in His provisions for them in Christ.

Trusting God to Meet the Needs

One of the impressive characteristics of Brother Harold's faith is his ability to simply trust God to meet the needs of the moment. After all, Jesus said, "Seek first the Kingdom of God and His righteousness and all these things will be added to you."

Jesus was talking about the daily material things we need in life. He was saying that we should not concentrate our main energy worrying about these things, but we should focus on seeking and doing God's will. When we do that, Jesus said that what we need would be given to us.

Brother Harold stated his conviction about God's supportive provision to a friend: "I believe if we are seeking to carry out a mission or ministry for the Lord Jesus, God will provide and equip us with all that we need to carry out that work for Him."

The Lord had provided a building for Youth Challenge at the corner of Crossland Avenue and Cumberland Drive. After Brother Harold looked over the building, he said to Jim, who was a co-worker, "We gotta get some games and things in here to attract and entertain young people."

Jim screwed up his face with a doubting grimace, "How're we gonna do that without any money? Pin ball machines and other things like that cost thousands of dollars."

"I don't know, Jim, but let's go out tomorrow looking and see what the Lord has for us. This is His work, not ours. I tell you what, meet me here at ten o'clock and we'll go looking in Nashville."

"Okay, but do you have enough money for gas?"

Brother Harold said, "Yeah, I got us covered for gas. See you tomorrow."

Harold and Jim left Clarksville around ten thirty to look for recreational equipment.

When they approached the city limits of Nashville, they saw a large amusement center store. Jim said, "Hey Harold, let's go in that place. It's huge and they must have all kinds of stuff. It'll give us an idea of what we'll need for our center"

The owner met them as they entered the building. He showed them rows of pinball machines, dartboards, shuffleboards and various types of entertainment equipment.

Harold asked the owner, "How much is this pin ball machine?"

"This simple one goes for five thousand five hundred and this more complex one sells for only seven thousand five hundred. How much do you want to invest?"

Harold said, "Sir, we only have fifty dollars."

"Fifty dollars!" the owner said, "that'll not even buy the legs on the machine."

Harold asked, "Sir, would you like to make an investment?"

"Investment? What kind of investment?"

"Sir, you can make an investment in the lives of hundreds of young people. We have a Youth Challenge Center in Clarksville and we need entertainment equipment to attract and to occupy young people to keep them off the streets and off drugs. Why don't you give us enough equipment to outfit our center?"

The owner looked at Harold with disbelief. "You come in here and I've never seen you before in my life and you want me to give you thousands of dollars worth of equipment?"

"Yes sir, I do. It's not for me. It's for hundreds of young people. It'll be the greatest investment that you've ever made in your life. Some young people's lives will be touched because you gave this pin ball machine and this other equipment."

"Listen, you guys. I've never given away anything in my life, and I don't intend to start now."

Jim and Harold started walking toward the building's exit. Just before they went out the door, the owner called to them: "If you show up with some trucks, I'll give you what you need. This is the craziest thing I've ever done. I don't know why I'm doing it, but I'm going too."

"Yes sir, thank you. We'll be back, as soon as possible, with some trucks to take the equipment to our youth center."

They pulled out and headed back toward Clarksville. Jim said, "Harold this is incredible. I've never seen anything happen like this. Does this happen with you often?"

Trusting God to Meet the Needs

"Jim, the Lord has given us what we need, when we need it, to carry out His mission. Praise the Lord! It's happened this way many times. I'm telling you, Brother, you gotta trust the Lord and He'll do unbelievable things for His people so that His name will be glorified."

"Brother Harold, praise the Lord that I could witness what just happened. Amazing, amazing. Now, Brother Harold, whatta we going to do about a truck? We don't know anybody who has a truck and we don't have enough money to rent a truck. But you know what? Somehow I believe that God will take care of that problem."

"That's the way to go Jim. Let's trust the Lord Jesus. Praise His Name!"

Jim and Harold passed a service station that had two U-Haul trucks, parked on beside of the station. "Jim, this is the place."

When Harold and Jim approached the station, the owner came out. "Can I help you men?"

Harold said, "Yes sir, you can. We need these two U-Haul trucks to haul some recreational equipment to Clarksville for our youth center."

"You men work with young people?"

"Yes sir, we do," Jim answered.

"We need more people like you to give time to our youth. I can't believe what's happening among our young people. You say you'll need both trucks?"

Harold said, "Yes sir, we do need both of them, but we don't have the money to pay for them. That amusement center that's about two miles from here on the left is going to give us all the equipment we need for the center. It's unbelievable that he's just going to give it to us."

The service station owner exclaimed, "You mean he just gave it to you?"

"Yes sir, now we need some trucks to haul the equipment to Clarksville. I believe the Lord is in all that's going on here."

The service station owner shook his head. "I would say that the Lord is in the middle of all this. I tell you what boys. Show me your driving license and I'm going to let you drive these trucks free of charge. It's for a great cause and I want to have a part in it."

Two hours later, Harold and Jim rounded up some young people to help them unload all the new equipment in the center. They left the center that morning with fifty dollars and a willingness to let the Lord lead them to fulfill their mission. They returned with fifty dollars, a stronger faith in the Lord who meets our needs for His glory, and a heart full of praise.

The Lilies of the Field

The Youth Challenge Center housed several young people who had been given to them from the courts. The center had no funding from the county, state or federal government; therefore, they had to provide food for the young people from their own resources.

Harold remembered, "One evening I received a complaint from the cook that they had plenty of vegetables, but no meat to serve. I took the complaint to the Board of Directors. One of the Board members, Charles Bryant, said that he had a beef cow that he would gladly donate to Youth Challenge."

Harold laughed as he told the story. He said, "Charlie giving one of his beef cows spurred the giving among the board members. Doyle Moore raised his hand and said, 'If Charlie Bryant can give a beef cow, than I can give one also'"

The next day, the game warden came by. He said, "Say, I've got two freshly killed deer that I want to give to Youth Challenge."

Harold said, "The Lord provided us with meat just when we needed it. God's timing is perfect."

At the following Saturday night Youth Challenge Rally, Harold shared with the audience how God had provided meat for the center. After the rally, Freely Riggins walked up to Harold and said, "I've got a dozen fat hens that I want to give to the center. The boys need some chicken to go with all that beef."

Harold said, "Thanks Freely. We'll really enjoy those fat hens. How about us coming out Saturday? Can we prepare the hens for cooking on the farm there?"

"Yeah, you city boys will need some help in getting the hens ready to eat."

The next Saturday Harold took the boys out to the Riggins farm. Freely showed the boys how to wring a chicken's neck. After Freely wrung the neck of two chickens, one of the boys tried his hand at it. The more he tried to wring the chicken's neck, the longer the neck became. Freely rescued the boy in his attempt to kill the chicken.

Finally, the dozen fat hens met their demise on a chopping block. The boys had never witnessed the killing of chickens, so their stomachs felt queasy. After the dozen hens were killed, they were lowed in a pot of hot boiling water, then the feathers were plucked off.

The next week the boys ate the beef hamburger, steaks and venison, but they would not eat chicken.

The cook told Brother Harold, "The boys ate the beef and venison, but they won't eat the chicken."

Brother Harold smiled, but he didn't say anything. He thought he knew why the boys passed up the chicken, so he asked one of the boys, "Why aren't you all eating chicken?"

The boy said, "Brother Harold, after we saw what those chickens have to go through to get on the table, it turned our stomachs."

The cook ended up having to make a lot of chicken casserole dishes for the boys.

The Youth Challenge Center lived on a tight budget. You might say that it operated day by day on faith, not knowing where the food was coming from or how the utilities were going to be paid.

One day Brother Harold laid all the bills out on the floor of the Center and called the boys to gather around and get on their knees to pray for the bills to be taken care of by someone, somehow.

While they were praying, Dr. Bill Corley came into the center. He asked, "What are you all doing?"

Brother Harold answered," We're praying for these bills to be paid. Come join us."

Dr. Bill Corley, pastor of the prestigious First Christian Church in Clarksville, knelt in prayer with Harold and the boys to pray for the bills to be paid.

Later on, when Dr. Corley told members of his congregation about this experience, some of them chided him: "Dr. Corley, you knelt on a dirty floor to pray with a bunch of wayward young people? After all, you're the pastor of the First Christian Church."

A few days later, Harold received a number of checks from members of Dr. Corley's church that paid all the bills. The pastor's bent knee impressed some people!

Youth Crusades

The Youth Challenge Center sent revival teams to churches and schools all over the Southeast. Hundreds of young people committed themselves to Christ in these meetings.

Harold and the Board of Directors for Youth Challenge visualized a Youth Crusade that would touch the youth of Clarksville. Even though it would cost several thousand dollars to conduct the crusade, they decided to go for it. They set the dates, May 4-9, 1970.

Harold visited many of the pastors in the city and county and tried to communicate his vision for the crusade to them. Many of them got on board with their support of the crusade.

The Board of Directors invited Paul Anderson, billed as the world's strongest man, to be one of the main speakers. Every night a prominent athlete gave his testimony. Bill Wade, former quarterback for the Chicago Bears, and Tony Romeo from the Boston Patriots, spoke during the week. Their testimonies impacted the young people for Christ.

Youth Crusades

Bill Morris, music director from the First Baptist Church in Clarksville, directed a youth choir. Special soloist, Ed Lyman, stirred the crowd each night with his heart-felt music.

The crusade was a tremendous success. Each evening Paul Andersen demonstrated his tremendous strength by lifting a table with eight men on it. After the demonstration, he gave a dynamic testimony. Every night the speakers challenged the crowd to commit their lives to Christ.

The fruit from the Crusade was one hundred and sixty youth and adults made commitments during the crusade.

After the Youth Crusade, Harold and Youth Challenge faced a summer full of opportunities and challenges. They could hardly imagine or project what lie before them.

For Harold, the summer and the events that took place, were deeply personal and would stir him to the depths of his being.

In 1969, York, Pennsylvania had been torn by riots. Police and firemen had been targeted and innocent citizens had become victims of stray bullets. An entire row of buildings had been burned in one chaotic, fury-filled night of racial riots.

When a girl slumped down in the street with two sniper bullets in her back, Harold Witmer returned to York, his hometown, to find that the girl was his sister. She was permanently paralyzed from the waist down. Harold felt that something had to be done to help the young people of York.

Now it was the summer of 1970, and the city of York was fearful of another summer filled with riots. Bill Shade, the Director of Teen Encounter, Inc., an evangelistic group, requested and received permission to conduct a citywide campaign of person-to-person evangelism.

Director Shade had approached the mayor with the prospect of this citywide campaign, knowing that the city had never permitted the use of a sound truck and was reluctant to permit open-air meetings.

The mayor not only granted a permit for the group to use a sound truck and hold night rallies, but he also granted the young people permission to use the city auditorium for a giant closing rally.

Youth Crusades

Bill Shade was ecstatic, because the mayor also gave permission for a parade. The City officials showed their confidence in the work of the young people.

During this time, Bill Shade called Harold and invited Youth Challenge to come to York to work with them in bringing the Gospel and revival to the city. In calling Harold to come to York was like asking a robbery victim to put up bail for the robber.

Harold's sister was paralyzed for life because of what happened in York. Now, they called him to be a Jonah to go to the Ninevites. Harold's love for the lost souls of York ruled over any bitterness toward the rioters who were responsible for the condition of his sister.

Harold was thrilled at the invitation to participate in person-to-person witnessing in downtown York. The Youth Challenge young people had already been trained in personal witnessing and they were ready to go.

After selecting those who were trained and willing to go, Harold arrived in York with twenty teenagers.

On the way to York, Harold had shared with the group the possible dangers that they could encounter. He read to them what Bill Shade had written to him: "I don't have to tell you that there is an element of danger involved in an operation like this. Let's agree together that God will have His hand upon the whole situation and use it for His glory, and that this city will not soon forget the impact that will be made upon it."

In the first few days of the evangelistic outreach, the young people struggled in their efforts to get out the Good News. During the morning hours, they prepared their literature for distribution, and in the afternoon they went out to do personal witnessing on the streets and parks.

Despite the efforts of the young people to share the Gospel, nothing happened. It seemed like a malaise had settled over the city. One group set up a literature display table and tract distribution center on Continental Square during shopping hours, but there was very little response.

Harold and the other leaders wondered if the people were afraid of another riot, or that the youth were unable to adapt to the new environment. So, they tried something different in order to relax the tension of the local population.

They played gospel music from the sound van, set up tables, chairs and gave out refreshments. Soon people of all ages started dropping by and chatting with them.

After a time of getting to know the people, they would ask, "Was there ever a time in your life when you trusted Christ Jesus as your personal Savior?"

This witnessing effort resulted in dozens of people trusting in Jesus as Savior and Lord. The witnessing campaign gained a new enthusiasm. At night, young people took the van into the troubled spots, where the year before houses had been burned down and people injured. Some Black Panther leaders were saved and also some longhaired hippies knelt to pray to invite Christ into their hearts.

Local churches began to experience the fires of revival as a warm, loving and enthusiastic spirit permeated their congregation. During the services every night, numbers of people came to the altar to pray.

Before the week was over, 333 people had prayed to receive Christ and many others had come to rededicate their lives to Christ in the churches.

To climax the witnessing effort, the youth staged a march with about a thousand people joining together, people of all ages and races. At the Saturday night rally, the city leaders stood to testify to the change they had witnessed in the city. They opened the city's parks to Teen

Encounter to begin open-air meetings on a regular basis. There were no riots in York that year. Praise the Lord!

Bill Shade's vision and action to carry it out, plus Harold's prepared young people and their readiness to go out and witness, produced fruit in York that will last forever.

A young girl from York wrote to the young people in Clarksville: "I have some good news for you. Thursday, when I walked through the square, Tom, a guy who got saved last week, asked why we didn't do this every day of the year. That shows God is going to save them yet. Five people had Holy Bibles, and were reading them, too. A few hippies were reading St. John. Isn't it great? Everyone in York is talking about how wonderful it is that people are getting involved with Christianity."

Revival had come to York, Pennsylvania!

The young people from Youth Challenge had gained experience in the York revival. They would have an opportunity to use this experience on the beaches of Florida.

Revival Comes to a Florida Beach

The plan to go to New Smyrna Beach to hold a revival was conceived and developed in Chicago. Brother Harold held a meeting in Chicago with Bill Corley, Mel Johnson and Doug Fisher at Addison Street Baptist Church.

One Saturday afternoon during the meetings, Doug invited the men to his house. While the men enjoyed their cold drinks and finger food, Doug shared with them: "A short time ago, I became the owner of a hotel in New Smyrna Beach which is located on the shores of the Indian River. The hotel needs to be renovated."

Brother Harold asked, "Doug, what are you going to do with that run-down hotel?"

"That's what I want to talk to you men about, Brother Harold. If you would bring teams to our town to hold meetings, the teams could also help renovate the hotel. Do you think this can be done?"

Bill Corley looked at Brother Harold, "You do have the youth who can do it, don't you?"

"Yeah, we can do it. We have fifteen or twenty young people who're ready to go at any time."

Doug said, "Great! That's a good number. Part of the group can help renovate the hotel and part of them can raise funds for the project."

When Brother Harold came back to Clarksville, he met with all the young people. "In a few more months I'm taking a team to New Smyrna Beach, Florida. I want each of you to begin to pray and seek to know if its God's will for you to go on this trip. If you go, you'll be called upon to help with the renovations, witness in the town and witness on the beach. How many of you are willing to go?"

Every hand in the group went up. There was a chorus of affirmation. "Brother Harold, we're ready any time. When do we go?"

"It will be several more months. You start praying about it and getting yourselves ready. I'll let you know the dates as soon as I know for sure."

The day came to tell the teens the departure date. Harold said to the group, "In order for you to qualify to go, you must be willing to work on the renovation project at the hotel, witness in the town of New Smyrna and on the beach. Every evening, after a day of work and witnessing, we'll gather in the lobby of the hotel for a time of praise and worship. You understand and still want to go?"

Again, a chorus, "Yes, we're right on with you, Brother Harold. We know how to do it, because we've done it before. No big deal. We'll have a revival!"

Brother Harold and the young people hit New Smyrna like a tornado. The quiet little town came alive. It would never be the same. After a few days of witnessing in the town and on the beach, the local newspaper carried a front-page write-up on the revival team's coming to New Smyrna.

A person visiting New Smyrna at this time could sense the excitement that permeated the town. During the first evening, a local policeman professed Christ as Lord and Savior. On the third night local pastors began to get involved.

The pastor of the First Nazarene Church, Rev. Chuck Acheson, invited the group to move the evening rallies from the hotel lobby to his church. The hotel lobby could no longer hold the overflowing crowd.

During the first night of the meeting in the church, a revival broke out that lasted thirty straight days.

While the team witnessed out on the beach, they met a young man whose family served in a prominent position in the church where the revival was in process. He had been backslidden for some time and wanted nothing to do with the church.

The young man was attracted by the excitement-taking place in the town and the happenings in his family's church. He wanted to see what was going on. He attended that night and the Holy Spirit dealt with this prodigal son in the way that a loving Father always deals with prodigals. He convicted him of living in the pigpen of sin and called him to turn his back on sins, repent, and go home to the Father. His life was dramatically changed.

This young man began to date one of the girls on the Youth Challenge Team. Later on they were married. Today, they still live in the New Smyrna area where they still serve Jesus.

After a month, the rally moved back to the hotel lobby. The meetings continued for the next eight years. Each year groups of young people would go for further training in evangelism. Incredible happenings were taking place month after month, and amazing stories were coming out of New Smyrna.

One of the young people in Youth Challenge, Dave Busby from Nashville, received an invitation from a large church in the Minneapolis area to come and teach his young people how to share Christ with the lost. Dave's ministry soon spread all over the metropolitan area.

Meanwhile, back in Clarksville, so many young people wanted to go to New Smyrna and get in on the excitement of the revival that Brother Harold had to rent a Greyhound bus to take them all. He made the trip three times a year with a busload of young people.

Revival came to New Smyrna Beach!

Trusting in the Crisis Moments

After the New Smyrna Beach and the other Florida revivals, Mel Johnson approached Harold: "Say Harold, how about us holding evangelistic meetings throughout the country? I mean going to the smaller towns that seldom or never have had an evangelistic crusade in their area."

"Mel, I haven't had any experience in speaking to large crowds of people, I'm not sure I'm prepared to do large meetings, but you've had experience with the Billy Graham Team, haven't you?"

"Yes, I worked with them for a while. I also did some work with the Oral Roberts Crusades. Now Harold, you've had experience holding evangelistic meetings with Youth Challenge. You've had some exciting and fruitful meetings. What do you think? Do you want to give it a try?"

"Sure Mel, I'll help you. You're Paul and I'm Timothy."

"You'll do great, Harold. We've already got an invitation to hold meetings in West Alexandra, Ohio. You know it's a small town near Hamilton, Ohio."

"Mel, what place will the meetings be held in?"

"We'll have a tent that will hold a thousand or more people."

"That's exciting Mel. Where's the tent now?"

"It's going to be delivered here to Clarksville. It'll have to be paid for on delivery."

"Paid for on delivery? We don't have any money. Mel."

Mel Johnson looked at Harold for several seconds. He said, "Harold, the Lord will provide."

Mel went back to Chicago to attend to some business. Several days later, the tent arrived on a large flatbed truck. The truck driver knocked on Harold's door. "You Mister Witmer? Got a tent for you. You owe a thousand dollars on it. Where do you want to unload it?"

Harold was stunned. There was the tent, but no money and no Mel. What could he do? They needed the tent, if they were going to have evangelistic crusades, but how could he pay for it?

Brother Harold

Harold got on the phone with Mel. "Mel, what am I going to do? The tent's here and I don't have a dime. The deliveryman wants his money now---a thousand bucks. Yeah Mel, I know the Lord will provide, but…but Mel, I don't have any money. You've got to go…go now? But Mel…"

The deliveryman was getting impatient. "Okay Mister, whatta ya going to do? Where do you want to unload it? I need to unload this thing and get some food and rest."

"Wait a minute, sir, before I can buy this tent, I've got to see it erected. I've got a friend who has a farm nearby. You follow me out there and I'll get some help and we'll erect the tent, then you can get back on the road."

Harold led the truck out to David Nussbaumer's farm. He sprinted up to the farmhouse door. "David, can we erect a tent on your land? It's not permanent. We just want to take a look to see if the tent is in good shape or not."

David asked, "What are you going to do with a tent, Harold?"

"We're going to be holding meetings over different states. A lot of people are going to get saved."

"Yeah Harold, no problem. You can put the tent up. Hey, I'll get you some help."

David enlisted the men who worked with him on the farm, and he called his neighbors and friends and invited them to help out with the tent. Word spread and within the next hour fifteen people gathered to help erect the tent. They were all needed, for it was not easy to erect a thousand-person tent.

While the tent was being erected, the men helping out began to get excited. "Harold, you say this tent will hold a thousand people? Where are you going to go?"

Harold said, "We're going to smaller towns that don't have large auditoriums. We'll pack this tent out and many people will be saved."

One of the men who came to help, Wendell Gannaway, said, "Harold, that sounds really exciting, but you don't look very excited."

"Wendell, a man in Bowling Green, Kentucky, Charles Rector, gave a large donation to buy the tent, but we're still a thousand dollars short. The delivery man standing over there wants the money before he can leave the tent."

Wendell Gannaway said, "I have the thousand dollars."

Once again Harold learned the lesson that if you're moving forward, on mission for the Lord Jesus, the Lord will supply your needs so that you can complete His work.

Harold and Mel took the tent all over Minnesota, Illinois and parts of Ohio. Many people came to trust Jesus as Lord and Savior because two evangelists claimed the promises of the Lord and launched out into the deep. People in Lake Crystal, Fairmont, Blue Earth, and Albert Lea, Minnesota still remember the big tent that came into town and the many lives that were changed because of their coming.

Harold and Mel learned some great spiritual lessons in those ten years of going back and forth from Tennessee to Minnesota. One lesson was that God uses the humblest and seemingly most insignificant people to advance His Kingdom cause.

One afternoon a fierce wind came across the plains of Minnesota and ripped the tent so badly that it seemed the meetings would have to be cancelled. Not so, for the farmers came out with their contact cement and canvass and patched the tent back together; and the meetings continued on.

Harold's heart was touched many times as he and Mel proclaimed the Gospel in the rural areas of Minnesota; but one incident touched him deeply. In the town of Blue Earth, a retired schoolteacher approached him. She said, "I have very little money at the present time, but I would like to put you in my will."

As time went by, Harold became more involved and busier than ever before; thus, he forgot about the schoolteacher.

Ten years passed. It was the Christmas season and Harold and Faye had no money for celebrating with their three children. Harold was reluctant to go to the post office to pick up their mail, because of the many bills that were coming in almost daily.

It's Christmas, you have a wife and three children and no money. That adds up to feelings of depression. Harold was not depressed, but he felt low and discouraged. He was about as low as he'd ever been in his life.

Brother Harold

One evening when Harold came home, Faye had picked up a stack of mail at the post office. There were so many letters that she had spread them on their bed, and the letters covered the entire space.

Faye said to Harold, "There's a letter from an attorney's office in Blue Earth, Minnesota. I think you need to give attention to it."

Harold reluctantly picked it up. "Maybe I've been sued by somebody up there."

When Harold opened the letter, it simply said that the lady schoolteacher, from Blue Earth, had passed away. She had left Harold four CDs each one worth five thousand dollars.

God had always brought people into Harold's life to help him in the hard times. God did it again.

Harold felt ashamed. He said, "I complained to God and told Him that I felt He had let me down. My wife and three children would have no presents and we would be scraping by just trying to eat. I told God that He had failed me, but the Lord has never failed me. I've failed Him, but He has always been faithful."

Faye said, "We had a great Christmas. Our hearts were full of joy, because the Lord had been faithful in supplying our needs. We were able to pay off all of our bills. God is good and faithful and that Christmas taught us to trust Him more and to claim His promises."

Adapting and Moving Forward

Brother Harold's early years in York, his time in the military, and his serving in the Christian Service Men's Center, had fine-tuned him to be flexible and open to the leadership of the Holy Spirit. He had experienced how exciting it is to follow the promptings and leadership of the Holy Spirit.

Now in 1974-75, Brother Harold faced a new problem that would test him to his limits. The Department of Human Services directed that the Youth Challenge Center have a full time residential social services director. The cost of hiring this new staff person would be more than the entire budget of the center.

After much prayer and deliberation, the Board of Directors agreed with Brother Harold that the only thing they could do was to close the center. It was a heart breaking development for Harold. The center had kept many young people off the streets and out of jail. It had also given spiritual and moral direction to hundreds of young people.

Adapting and Moving Forward

Brother Harold, in order to support his family, went into the business of repairing car bumpers with his friend, Al Johnson. His new business called upon him to travel all over the region to sell the bumpers. He spent a lot time in Chicago and other northern states.

While in the Chicago area, he enjoyed a time of fellowship with his friend, Mel Johnson, an evangelist and former member of the Board of Directors for Youth Challenge. During this time with Mel, they planned and held revival meetings in Minnesota, Ohio, Tennessee, Kentucky, Indiana and Illinois.

At that time, the Lord impressed Brother Harold to start a new evangelical ministry. In sharing his vision with some fellow Christians, he found that the same desire was aflame in their hearts also.

The first announcement for the founding of a new evangelical ministry was given at a Thanksgiving banquet held at the New Providence Methodist Church in Clarksville, in 1975. After that announcement, a group of interested people met at Lonzo's Seafood Restaurant on College Street. The Community Church of Clarksville, Tennessee, was birthed from that meeting.

The Lord led Brother Harold Witmer, Davis Lee Potts, Jim Hancock, W.B. Austin, Wendell Gannaway and Dr. William Corley to meet together for the purpose of establishing the first interdenominational church in the Clarksville area. These men prayed for God's direction in the selection of leaders for the new church.

The original constitution of the church stated the purpose of the church: "The purpose of this church is revealed in the New Testament, to win people to faith in Jesus Christ as Lord and Savior and to see that they become active disciples in His Church, the Bride of Christ."

The first public worship service for the new church was held on December 28, 1976, at the Ed Norman National Guard Armory. From that simple beginning, services have continued every Sunday morning, Sunday evening and Wednesday night since that opening worship service.

The leadership of the Community Church called Dr. Bill Corley to be their pastor. Dr. Corley resigned his position of pastor of the First Christian Church to assume the role of pastor of the newly founded Community Church.

Adapting and Moving Forward

Leaving his position as pastor of the First Christian Church certainly was an act of faith on Dr. Corley's part, since he had no assurance of a salary. Not only was he not sure of a salary, he left the spacious parsonage of the First Christian Church not knowing if he would have a new place to live. Brother Harold said, "Brother Bill took a step of faith when he accepted the invitation to be the pastor of a newly organized church."

In a few weeks the newly formed congregation bought Dr. Corley and his wife, Barbara, a new house that was to be the parsonage.

A short while after the church had started, Brother Harold and Dr. Corley were driving down Highway 41A. Dr. Corley pointed to a large plot of land. "Harold, stop the car! This is where we'll build the church."

Brother Harold said, "Brother Bill this land sells by the inch not by the foot."

Dr. Corley repeated, "Harold, this is where we'll build the church."

Dr. Bill Corley's inspiration of the moment had to have come from the heavenly places where God reveals His counsels to seeking and faithful hearts.

Before the day was over, Dr. Corley's belief that the church would be built on that expensive plot of land across from Gate One at Ft. Campbell was affirmed.

Harold and Dr. Corley inquired about the ownership of the land. They were directed to the house of Bud Fisher. Dr. Corley said to Mr. Fisher, "When we passed by your land, something jumped in my heart and I feel strongly that this is where God wants us to build our new church."

"Tell me about the church you want to build."

Harold and Dr. Corley shared with Bud Fisher their vision of a church that would touch soldiers, businessmen and hundreds of others in the area.

Dr. Corley asked, "Mr. Fisher, how much do you want for the land?"

Bud Fisher did not answer immediately. He looked upward over the two men standing before him. He seemed to see something that no one else could see. Finally, he answered, "Preacher, you know what? I think I'll just give you two acres to build your church on."

Bud Fisher, the owner of the land, did give two acres for the building of the church. God began moving in a mighty, miraculous way in response to His children's prayers of faith.

The moving of the Lord in a miraculous way continued. In the Sunday morning service, it was suggested that the church needed to buy the remaining eleven acres joining the two acres that the church had just received as a gift. One of the elders said, "We can't buy the land now, we don't have the money."

The next morning a lady who had, the previous day, visited the church for the first time, came into the temporary church office and handed Dr. Bill Corley a check for the entire amount of the land. God is able.

Harold spoke about the provision of God for those who lay their lives on the line to do His will. He said, "Don't think of anything else; just focus only on winning people to Christ and God will provide all your needs to carry out your mission."

On October the 4th, 1976, a groundbreaking ceremony was held as the congregation prepared to build a simple metal structure that would be used for worship services and the other activities of the church. The building has over seventeen thousand square feet and is located at 199 Jack Miller Boulevard, next to Clarksville's Municipal Airport.

If you visit the Community Church on Sunday morning, you will see all races and all nationalities. You will see soldiers, businessmen, students, children, seniors and people who are living on the margin of life. You will feel the welcome extended to everyone and you will feel loved. Those are evidences of the presence of God's Spirit!

A Wild Plane Ride: Safe By the Grace of God

God touched the hearts of several people, and they gave the land for the building of the Community Church. One of the first things needed for the erection of a building was a concrete slab.

Harold and a friend from Atlanta, Bob Draper, undertook the job of pouring the cement for the slab. Bob was a commercial concrete layer and finisher. While they were in the process of pouring the cement, Bob received word that his mother had passed away in Valdosta, Georgia.

Bob wanted to leave immediately, but Brother Harold counseled that they needed to finish pouring the cement. Brother Harold said, "Bob, if we don't finish pouring the slab, we'll have to dig it up and start over again."

"I know that's true Brother Harold, but I've got to be there for my mother's funeral."

"Let's pour the slab, Bob, and then we'll use the Tri-pacer airplane that was given to us, to fly to Valdosta.

Al's a pilot and he can fly it. We'll fly that Tri-pacer straight to Valdosta in a few hours, okay?"

"Sounds good. Let's hurry and finish."

Before they resumed pouring the cement, Brother Harold sent word to Al to prepare the plane for a flight to Florida. They finished pouring the slab, and early the next morning they boarded the Tri-pacer for the flight to Valdosta. The trip during the daylight hours went without incident.

They arrived in plenty of time for Bob to spend time with his family and to prepare for the funeral service. After the graveside service, Brother Harold said to Bob, "We need to get on back to Clarksville and finish with the concrete while everything there is still in place."

Al was standing nearby. He said, "I've gassed up the plane and she's ready to go."

By the time they took off, it was late afternoon. When they came near Atlanta, it was completely dark. Bob was sitting in the back passenger seat. He nudged Brother Harold, "Hey, something's wrong. A few minutes ago Atlanta was on our right and now Atlanta is on our left."

A Wild Plane Ride: Safe By the Grace of God

Harold looked at the instrument gauges. They indicated that they were flying in circles. Harold said to Al, the pilot, "Hey Al, we have problems. We're flying in circles."

Al rubbed his eyes. "I have a terrible migraine headache and all I can see are flashes of light in front of me."

Brother Harold knew then that they had to get the plane on the ground. They were lost. They could not land at the Atlanta International Airport. They had to find a smaller airport. Harold said to Bob, "Hey look for a white and green blip going through the sky. That will be a smaller airport."

In a few minutes Bob shouted, "Look, there's a small airport."

Harold said to Al, "See the lit runway? Line her up and take her down."

As the plane approached, Harold shouted to Al, the pilot, "Hey, take this thing up. You're heading it into the tower."

After the pilot make several approaches, it became obvious that he could not land on the lit runway. Bob who was in the back seat asked no one in particular, "Do these little planes have parachutes? If they do, I'm jumping out."

Brother Harold said, "Bob, there's no parachutes in small planes."

Bob cried out to his newly deceased mother, "Mother, I'm coming to see you!"

The plane made another pass around the airport. Bob located a swamp on the backside of the airport. He said, "Let's take it down in that swamp. We're running out of gas. Look at those gas gauges. We've gotta take it down now!"

Harold instructed Al, "Take her down in that swamp."

When the plane came over the swamp, Al still could not see. As the plane made an approach over the swamp, Harold said, "This is about as close as you can get. Take her down now!"

Al refused to land toward the runway, but he finally brought the plane to land on a grassy strip at the end of the runway. Planes are usually parked on this strip, but fortunately the planes had been moved for a construction project.

A Wild Plane Ride: Safe By the Grace of God

When the plane hit the freshly dug ditches, mud flew everywhere. The plane finally came to a halt on one of the turning lanes. They taxied the plane over to the tower where a policeman stood waiting for them. The tower had phoned for the police, after the plane had made several passes over the airport.

When the three had lit from the plane, the policeman walked over and said to them, "Gentlemen, that was one of the most beautiful landings I have ever seen. Is there anything I can do for you?"

Harold said, "Yes sir, there is. We would like to spend the night. Can you tell us where there's a motel?"

"I sure can. There's one nearby. I know the owner. Come on, get in my car and I'll take you there."

The next morning the motel owner drove them to the airport. Arriving at the airport, they saw their plane caked with mud, gassed up and ready to go. The day was beautiful and the crew looked forward to a safe trip; however, when they neared Tullahoma, Tennessee, the sky turned completely dark and ice started to appear on the wings and front of the plane.

Al took the plane lower to try to get under the dark cloud mass. Right below was an abandoned bomber base from World War 11 days. The runways were still in great shape and there were no planes sitting on them.

Brother Harold told Al, "Sit her down in the middle of those runways."

While they were taxing up the runway, Brother Harold said to his two traveling companions, "It's only by the goodness and grace of the Lord that we've made it this far. Let's leave the plane here and take a bus back to Clarksville."

Faye met them at the bus station in Clarksville. She had been praying, "Lord, keep them safe in the palm of Your hand."

It was only later that she realized how much her prayers were needed and how much they had been answered.

That was the last trip Harold ever made in a small plane.

Bibles to the Russians

In 1992, a prayer meeting that took place in Clarksville, at the First Baptist Church, resulted in a commitment to start a church in East Fulga, Western Germany. Charles Currie, a former chaplain, told of the great need there. After his tour as a chaplain, he had gone back and served in West Germany in 1988-89. He said, "A person can go into East Germany with cookies and Bibles and they will receive them."

A group from Clarksville went to West Germany with Brother Currie and started a ministry in Fulda and other areas.

Brother Currie had Bibles printed in Russian at a publishing company in Kentucky and brought them to Clarksville; however, that year, 1993, no one from Clarksville could return to Germany.

Harold Witmer had heard Chaplain Currie speak and had kept up with the team that had gone to Germany. He knew of the Russian Bibles that were brought to Clarksville, and that a team would not be going back in 1993.

One night during that time, Harold was lying in bed and tears came streaming down his face. Faye recalled the moment, "Tears were just streaming down his face." She said, "Harold, is anything wrong with you? Are you sick?"

"I see the Russian soldiers reaching for Bibles and there's no one to give Bibles to them." Harold said with a choking voice.

Faye said, "Harold, why don't you go and do it?"

Later on, Dr. Bill Corley further confirmed God's leadership in the matter of Harold going to Germany. He said, "Harold, why don't you go?" He turned and said to several members of the church, "Let's ship Harold outta here."

Harold committed to go to East Germany and to take as many Bibles as possible.

Faye decided to go with Harold. Later Pastor Otis Ramsey, Andrew and Juanita Thompson, Zandra Darnell, Pat Lamb and Earl Baggett decided to go, also. Carol Golla from Minnesota heard about the trip and sent word that she wanted to go and would meet the team in Chicago, at the airport.

Bibles to the Russians

Even though Harold had committed to go take Bibles to the Russian soldiers and people, he didn't know the Russian language, and he didn't even know where they were going in East Germany. He didn't have the slightest idea of how he was going to get the Bibles to the Russians, but he knew God was in it. He also believed God would provide all their needs.

In getting ready for the trip, the team packed sixteen duffle bags full of sweaters, and Christian literature. Two cartons of Bibles were also added to the accompanying baggage. Each team member would have two duffle bags to check in.

At the airport in Nashville, Harold and the team members were concerned about the duffle bags getting through okay. Seventy pounds was the limit per person. They had not weighed the bags, but knew that some of them were rather heavy. Harold said, "We may have to repack some of these bags."

Harold sent the heaviest bags through first. All but three were on or slightly under the limit. The American Airline Desk Manager became curious and interested in what was going on. Harold explained to the manager, "We're taking sweaters, other goods and Bibles into East Germany. We're a Christian group from Clarksville."

"Hey, that's wonderful," said the manager "Send all the bags through. It's okay."

God had provided the first person to help the team along the way. Others would come into their lives further on in Germany.

The team left Nashville and flew to Chicago where they met Carol Golla at the airport. From Chicago they flew to Dusseldorf and then on to Berlin.

On the flight, Faye turned to Harold and said, "The others on the team think you know what you're doing, but I know you don't."

"Well, God does and we'll just have to trust Him to see us through."

When they arrived in Berlin, they only had the name of a recreational center. Colonel Dees, a Chaplain at Ft. Campbell, had wired the center and made reservations for them.

In the Berlin airport, they were a bit overwhelmed. They had sixteen duffle bags and two cartoons of Bibles and not the slightest idea where the recreational center was located or how they would transport all their baggage there.

Harold saw a US Army soldier standing nearby. He asked him, "Do you know where the recreation center is located?"

"Yeah, I know. I can take you there."

"You don't understand. We have a lot of baggage."

The soldier said, "You don't understand. I have a bus. I came to pick up a group of soldiers who didn't show up. I can take all of you and your bags. No problem."

God provided the bus that took them to the recreation center where they were to stay.

After checking in the hotel, Harold, Andrew and Juanita Thompson took a train to pick up the two leased vehicles. Only a nine-passenger van was available, and it was large enough to accommodate all the needs of the team.

It took Harold and the Thompson's three hours to find their way back to the hotel. By that time, the other team members had unpacked all the bags and had sorted out the literature, sweaters and Bibles. After Harold and the Thompsons arrived, they all went to eat at a nearby restaurant.

The team saw the hand of God at work for them in coming thus far; they continued to see His leadership in the following days in East Germany.

A Warm Response in a Cold Setting

How and where could they go to give out Bibles to the Russians? That question came to the mind of every team member.

The hotel provided breakfast and a large meeting room for the team. After a satisfying meal, the team boarded the van. Harold said, "I didn't know where to go. I handed Faye a map and told her to find the way to Potsdam where the Russian Military Hospital was located."

Just at that time a Russian Army convoy passed in front of the hotel. Harold told the driver, "Follow that convoy!"

The convoy led them to the Russian area where a guard was on duty. Harold offered him one of the team's jackets, but the guard refused. The guard pointed to the area to the right. The team loaded their bags with Russian Bibles and drove to the area where there was building after building.

The buildings were pre-World War11, five stories with two apartments in each stairwell. The people were surprised to see Americans handing out Russian Bibles and literature, but accepted the Bibles with smiles and thanks.

Faye said, "When we had given out all of our Bibles and literature, we went back to the van. The guard had already assembled the rest of the team together and told them they must leave. We all were ready to leave for we had given out all the materials we had brought with us"

A young Russian who spoke English said to the team, "How did you get inside these apartments? Even Russians do not have access to get in here."

He was not aware that the Lord opens doors that man cannot possibly open.

Harold asked the young English-speaking Russian, "Where is another area that we can go to give out literature?"

"You go down this road to a church," he said, "They will tell you where to go."

Going down the road, they came to a Russian Orthodox Church. It was small but beautiful. It looked more like a shrine than a building that was used. The priest lived in a two-story log house nearby. They met a tourist from Belgium who interpreted for them. He told them that the Russian hospital was south of Potsdam just off the Autobahn near Beelitz.

When the team arrived, it was dusk. Nearby was a bus stop outside of the busy gates. Harold said, "We handed out Bibles and literature to everyone at the gates and took off into the camp. No one stopped us."

The team split into twos and went in different directions. There was a huge building in the center of the area. They went from door to door. Faye said, "We went into this large room that was a café. Everyone wanted a Bible. We all had to go back to the van several times to get more Bibles and literature."

One of the two person teams had gone into a children's hospital. The nurses gave them white coats to wear while they were giving out literature to the children and their parents. When the Russian doctor arrived, he told them to leave.

Another team went into a large kitchen area where a number of cooks were working. They all wanted a Bible.

The full team met at the van and headed down toward Beelitz. They stopped at a bus stop where there was a wall that had a break in it. People were going in and out. There they handed out a large number of Bibles.

Going a little further down the road, they came to a housing area. There they, again, handed out a large number of Bibles.

The next morning the team left for Slubice, Poland to give out Bibles in the Polish language. A guard stopped them at the bridge that connected Slubice with their sister city in Germany, Frankfort der Oder. They had to park in Frankfort on der Oder, and carry the Bibles across the bridge for three or four more blocks.

Harold said, "The weather was very cold. We took the Bibles across the bridge and set up at a taxi stand in Slubice."

Faye recalled, "Carol and I went into a restroom in a seedy looking hotel. We had to go through a bar/restaurant to get to the restroom. In coming back through, we tried to give out Bibles. No one wanted them. Finally, one guy understood the Bibles were free, and then everyone wanted one. We gave out all of the Bibles we had with us."

They also went into the shopping areas to give out Bibles in the pubs, butcher shops and restaurants. People

A Warm Response in a Cold Setting

were reluctant to take them, until they found out that they were free; then everyone wanted them.

When they had given out all the Bibles and children's literature, Harold and Earl walked five blocks back across the bridge to get more Bibles to reload their bags.

One Polish-speaking man from Canada asked the team, "Why are you doing this? Are you missionaries?"

Carol answered, "No, we do it because we care about where people will spend eternity."

When it got late and dark, they took a taxi back to the Polish border crossing. Pat Lamb discovered she had misplaced her passport. Even though the Polish guards let her through, the German guards at the German border would not let her in without a passport.

A German guard took her to the main station house. Faye said, "While waiting at the main station house, we saw a bus waiting for clearance. I found out that they all spoke Polish, so Carol and I grabbed our bags and boarded the bus to give out our remaining Bibles. When the first person we gave a Bible too, told the others that it was a Bible and they were free, then everyone on

117

the bus wanted one. We gave out all the Bibles plus all the children's literature."

In the meantime, Pat found out that her passport had been tucked in the sweater sleeve that Zandra was carrying. The guards allowed Zandra to come to the border and give Pat her passport.

Faye said, "We decided that God must have wanted that bus load to get Bibles which could not have happened if we had not had to wait."

The following morning Spec Carlos Rivera arrived before the team arose for the day. Rivera spoke fluent German. The army assigned him to drive and interpret for them. He went to get gas while the team ate their breakfast.

On the way to Dresden, the team was delayed because of an accident on the Autobahn. While the cars were stopped, the team passed out tracts and children's literature.

When the way was clear, the team went on to Dresden. They located John Noble's castle. Harold spoke about John Noble, "John came and spoke in Clarksville several times. While in Clarksville, we got to know him and became friends."

John's father grew up in Dresden, but moved to Detroit in the 1920s. The family moved back to Dresden, in the 1930s to be near the hot springs there. They bought a camera company that became successful. The Germans permitted the company to operate during the war. When the Russians came in 1945, they accused his father, Charles, and John of being spies and sent them to prison. John's father, Charles died in 1952.

John's imprisonment was brought to President Eisenhower's attention in 1955, and he secured John's release. After his release, John Noble wrote, *I was a Slave in Russia*, and, *I found God in Soviet Russia*. John went on speaking tours and became well known among Christian and political conservatives.

After the team arrived in Dresden, they located the Noble family castle. John warmly welcomed them and prepared a delicious meal for the team. Later on they had a worship service together. John shared his testimony with them. Faye said, "It was a moving experience."

On the way back to Berlin, the van ran out of gas on the Autobahn. Carlos called for assistance. Before help arrived, Earl Baggett took off, unannounced, to find gas. The Emergency Team said there was no gas within fifty kilometers, but Earl came back with 20 liters, even though he was unable to speak a word of German. He went to a village just off the Autobahn and used hand language to get his message across.

On Monday the team headed back to Beelitz. On the way, they passed a stalled Russian convoy. They stopped and handed out Bibles to the soldiers. They continued on to a Russian base with three gates deep Harold drove the van up to a guard. He had to go to the guardhouse for a pass. Pastor Otis Ramsey said to Harold, "Please, Brother Harold. Don't go on to the guards. They may arrest us here."

Harold said to the guard, "We want to go in and hand out Bibles to the soldiers."

The soldier stood firm in front of Harold, "Nein, nein. No can do that."

"God has sent us here to bring Bibles to Russian soldiers."

The guard said, "Whose authority you come?"

"God has sent us!"

A Warm Response in a Cold Setting

Harold took a Bible and put one of their caps on top of it and gave it to the soldier. "Here's a gift to you."

"A gift to me? A present? You enter!"

The van drove through the gate and went down for several blocks until they saw a platoon of soldiers. They stopped and handed out Bibles to them. The soldiers broke rank and crowded around the van to get the Bibles. All of the Bibles were handed out.

Just when they finished handing out the Bibles, the Russian lieutenant guard rushed up on a bicycle. He got off his bike and held up his hand. He stumbled several times in his attempt to communicate in English. Finally, he said, "How you say 'not allowed?'"

The team had completed its mission, so they smiled and saluted the Lieutenant and got back into their van to drive back to the hotel. God is good!

On Wednesday the team flew back to Nashville. They were full of the joy that people feel when they carry out a mission of sharing the Gospel of Jesus Christ with those who are lost.

Another Vision, Another Ministry

Harold ministered as one of the pastors of Community Church. In that role, he soon became the chairman of the missions committee. For those who knew Harold, that was no surprise, for God had placed the whole world on his heart. His vision was larger than Clarksville and America.

In order to have a platform to launch a ministry that was nation and world wide, Harold activated Christian Partners. The Christian Servicemen's Center formerly operated under this umbrella. This organization worked with churches all over the USA to reach out in ministry to needs, both physical and spiritual. It also reached out to other countries to share the Gospel of Jesus Christ.

Christian Partners was the platform that Harold used to launch his ministry to the Russians in the Kaluga area, to send tile to the orphanages in Moscow, medical supplies to Haiti, Mexico, Jamaica, India and to China.

Christian Partners sponsors six orphanages in Russian. It helps fifteen others. They bought a 125-acre farm 180 miles south of Moscow which ministers to 700 plus children, recovering alcoholics, drug addicts and the community surrounding them.

Harold spoke of one of the roles of Christian Partners: "We like to work with large or small churches, especially the small churches. Many of these churches have no vision of worldwide missions. When one or two of their members go on a mission trip with us, they are changed and they bring a new vision back to their church. We join with these churches to carry the Gospel around the world."

In 1994, Harold wanted to go back to East Germany to give out more Bibles to the Russian soldiers; however, he found out that the Russian soldiers had all gone back to Russia.

Harold had a thousand Russian Bibles printed and in his possession. He needed to go to Russia to give them out. God opened the door for him to go into Russia. "Revival Fires" out of Branson, Missouri, invited Harold and a team to go with them to Colomna, Russia.

Hubert White, a retired master sergeant, Charles Currie, a retired chaplain, and Pastor Otis Ramsey composed the team to go with Harold. They arrived in

Colomna on a cool, overcast day and checked in their hotel to get some sleep before they launched out on their evangelistic activities.

Colomna is a beautiful city with a population of 146,000. A high red brick wall encircles a portion of the city. The city is located at the confluence of the Moskva and Oka Rivers. The city fathers have emphasized their past history by renovating several old castles and buildings of historical significance. Tall church steeples tower over parts of the city from the Russian Orthodox churches.

The next morning, after a Russian breakfast with plenty of black coffee, the team went to the trolley and bus' main terminal to hand out Bibles. They were surprised at how friendly and receptive the Russian were to the handing out of Bibles. The first day they handed out more than half of their Bibles, and other literature.

The response was so good that the team set up a PA system and preached there every day while handing out New Testaments.

Several Russians who spoke some English made conversation with them and thanked them for coming to Russia. One of these Russians, a Russian submarine commander who spoke good English, attached himself to the team and spent time with them every day. They filmed several of his stories.

This openness and freedom was just after the Berlin Wall came down. The team could hold services in schools, public-gathering places and just about anywhere they wanted to go, at that time. It was the right time to be in Russia.

The second day, they finished giving out the Bibles. The team was disappointed that they didn't have more Bibles. It was only the second day and they had already handed out all their Bibles. It looked like it might, from then on, be a disappointing trip.

But one of the members of the "Revival Fires" team had contacts that saved the day. His contact in Colomna got him in touch with a publishing company that could get Russian Bibles.

After a day's wait, the team bought two thousand more Russian Bibles, to give out. They headed back to the main station and to the market place to complete their mission.

The team gave out Bibles on the streets, market places, stores, pubs and shops in the city. Over all, the people were receptive and pleased to receive a Bible.

In three more days the Bibles were all given out. The team was ecstatic over the reception and success of the mission. They knew that the Word of God would not return void. Thousands of Russians could read God's Word in their own language. Many Russians had never owned a Bible or read or heard the Gospel News of Jesus Christ.

This was a memorable day for the people in Colomna, Russia, for they had had no communication with Americans for more than fifty years. Then, all of a sudden, Americans with red jackets were handing out Bibles at the main station and market place. The people were surprised and blessed by this turn of events.

Hubert White spoke about this trip: "This was my first trip. Was I ever blessed! Really, I was hooked on this trip. I went back to Russia with Brother Harold eight straight times. I wouldn't trade the experiences for anything."

That trip kindled the fire in Brother Harold's heart, a fire of burning desire to bring the Gospel to the Russian people.

The Kaluga Experience

Chuck and Cecil Todd of "Revival Fires" again invited Harold to go with them to Russia. The target city, this time, was Kaluga, located 120 miles south of Moscow.

Hubert White, a retired master sergeant, also went with Harold.

The team arrived in Moscow with their duffle bags full of Bibles and Christian literature in the Russian language. The bags went through customs without a hitch. Praise the Lord!

Arrangements had been made for a bus to take them to Kaluga. After the duffle bags were loaded on the bus, they were on their way to Kaluga.

After arriving in Kaluga, the team checked into a hotel in the downtown area. They showered and made preparation to eat dinner at one of the local restaurants. The steaks were somewhat tough, but tasty enough served with a baked potato.

The next morning Harold and Hubert went out looking for a place to rent to hold evangelistic meetings. They passed a movie theater that had a sign on it in

Russian. From all appearances it looked like the owners were trying to rent the building. They were right!

Going into the theater, they met the owner. Fortunately, he spoke enough English, so they were able to get their message across. They rented the building for seven nights.

The mornings and afternoons before the meetings, the team handed out flyers inviting the public to attend. They also handed out Bibles on the streets and in the market place, inviting those who received them to attend the services at the rented movie theater.

The first night, only a few adults and young people showed up for the meeting. The meeting was conducted through an interpreter. Harold and Hubert were disappointed at the attendance, but they remained determined to go all out to proclaim the Gospel in Kaluga.

Each night the attendance increased. On the fourth night, the theater filled with mostly children and young people.

The Russian adults were very cautious about associating with Americans.

On the fifth night, a Russian pastor, Pastor Grigori, came early to the theater with six members of his local congregation. Through his broken English and hand signals, he conveyed, "I want to help you reach the local people here. I can interpret and we can sing special songs and give testimonies in Russian."

Harold said, "We embraced Pastor Grigori then and there. He was God-sent. From the fifth night on, the theater was packed out."

During the meetings, fifty to sixty people made professions of faith. Pastor Grigori and his church followed up on them.

Harold said, "When the meetings were over, we met with Pastor Grigori in his one bedroom apartment. He shared with us his vision of reaching Russia with the Gospel of Jesus Christ. His vision resonated in our hearts and minds. In that moment we bonded with Pastor Grigori in his efforts to reach Russia for Jesus."

Pastor Grigori said, "We want you to come back next year. We'll have meetings in homes, as well as the theater."

The following year, Harold and Hubert White came back with an all-star team:

Steve Robinson, Director of the Fellowship of Christian Athletes for the State of Tennessee; Bill

Harrison, stock broker in Nashville; Chuck Currie, retired military chaplain; Dr. Hal Hadden, Bible teacher and Vanderbilt graduate.

Harold remembered the team's efforts as they met in homes and at the theater with Pastor Grigori and his church participating: "It was a great evangelistic outreach! We touched hundreds of people. Many people came to experience Christ."

Pastor Grigori said, "In another year, a thousand people will be meeting in the movie theater."

Christian Partners, together with Community Church and a number of other churches, teamed up with Pastor Grigori to buy the movie theater and to turn it into a large facility for worship and training. Today they have a thousand in attendance.

Every year in May, a Christian Partners Team leaves from the Nashville Airport to go to Kaluga to work together with Pastor Grigori in starting new churches and strengthening the existing churches. They have started thirty new churches, so far.

The Kaluga experience is an on-going experience. Dr. Steve Witmer, Harold and Faye's son, now is directing the Russian work in Kaluga. He works together with

Pastor Grigori. The work is still growing and new missions are being established and new ministries launched to assist the new churches.

Pastor Grigori communicated his vision to Harold that day in his one bedroom apartment. That vision has and is being carried out for the glory of God.

A Trip Realized

I, the author of this book, had wanted to go to Russia with Harold and his team back in the nineties, but my desire was not realized. After years of service in Vietnam, Philippines, Indonesia and Zambia, Gloria and I were led to serve in Bratislava, Slovakia. While in Bratislava, Harold communicated with me about the possibility of my joining him and his team in Kaluga, but I could not because of commitments to the mission in Slovakia.

After Gloria and I retired, the opportunity came to go with Harold and the Christian Partner Team in 2003. Gloria encouraged me to go.

Harold had asked me to raise money to buy Russian Bibles to take with us. The tremendous generosity of Christian friends in Brownsville, Tennessee will always be remembered as they gave enough money to buy four thousand Bibles to take with us. John and Emma Jane Gorman, beloved friends who have gone on now to be with Jesus, led out in getting the money together.

Brother Harold

On May 1, 2003, the Christian Partner Team gathered at the airport in Nashville. For the first time I met Hubert White, Melinda Potts Ross, Kathy Wilcox, Jim LeBrec, Kathy Tremblay, Tom and Marty Parker, Stu Martin and a friend from Texas.

Harold had a duffle bag full of Bibles, children's literature and goodies for the orphans for each one of us to carry as luggage.

For me, it was a happy time of meeting new friends on the team and anticipating the mission venture into Russia.

At the airport, I noticed that all the team members had on a red jacket with the American flag emblazoned on the right arm and the USA over the top pocket. My first response was one of doubt about wearing such a flashy looking jacket. Bad guys could spot us a mile off.

Later on, during the trip, I saw the wisdom of wearing the red jacket with the American flag and USA on it. First of all, at the airport in Moscow, they treated us like celebrities. We were put first in line at immigration and customs. Our bags were expedited through in record time. Secondly, we could spot one another in a crowd and keep in contact.

A Trip Realized

After checking through immigration and customs at the airport, a bus loaded us and headed out for Kaluga. It would take around four hours to get to our destination. The four-hour plus drive through the Russian countryside gave an opportunity to see the farms and rural setting. It was a beautiful drive.

Especially interesting to me was to see the large sunflower fields where farms grew hundreds of acres of the giant sunflowers to be marketed for their seeds to make oil. Russia is one of the top producers in the world of sunflower seeds and sunflower seed oil.

In the middle of Saturday afternoon we arrived in Kaluga and checked in our hotel. The women on the team brought several duffle bags full of healthy foods, and the hotel provided us with a dining room and kitchen. Each morning we ate breakfast at the hotel, and sometimes we ate lunch there, also. Dinner would be eaten out in some restaurant, with each person responsible for his meal.

Sunday morning was the Russian Christian Easter Sunday morning. Their Easter is the first Sunday in May. We were going to celebrate Easter with the Community Church led by Pastor Grigori. Late Saturday evening,

Harold had asked, "Joe, would you bring the Easter message? You'll preach through an interpreter."

"Yeah, I'll be glad too. I have a message with me that I preached two weeks ago in Alabama."

When we arrived at the church, it was already packed out. A fellowship meal had been planned following the morning service. The greeting, "He has risen!" was heard throughout the auditorium. And the response, "He has risen, indeed!" was the resounding reply to the greeting. The service was all in Russian, but we did understand the greetings because we had been prepped on the words.

The singing in the worship service rang out over the auditorium. The Russian people love to sing. One of members of our team gave a testimony through an interpreter.

My fifteen-minute sermon, in English, lasted thirty minutes with the Russian interpretation. I wish I had cut it down to ten minutes. Brother Harold had cautioned me about being too long. When the invitation was extended, no one came to the altar.

Later on, in the evening service, Brother Harold preached a fifteen-minute sermon, including interpretation. When he gave the invitation, twenty to thirty people came to the altar.

The next morning, after breakfast and our devotional time, we left the hotel at ten o'clock to visit our first orphanage. Christian Partners sponsors six orphanages and helps support a number of others. We had two interpreters to interpret for us. Tatiana, in her twenties, and Elena, in her forties, were both very helpful in bridging the gap between English and Russian.

The orphans were prepared for our coming. They had planned a program for us and we also had a program to follow them. They sang several Russian folk songs and then two ten-year-old girls did a ballet dance. A teenage girl sang *Yesterday* in English. After the programs we opened the duffle bags, which were full of goodies, books and clothes and gave them out to the orphans. It was a grand time.

One of the highlights of our program for the orphans was Stu Martin singing his country-western songs. Stu is six foot-two, wears jeans, cowboy boots and a cowboy hat. The orphans loved him and wanted his autograph. He was a hit wherever he went in Russia.

Brother Harold

The next morning after breakfast and our devotion, Harold announced our schedule for the day. "We're going to the market and to hand out Bibles. We have four thousand Bible, so it will take several days to hand them out."

I paired up with Stu Martin, as we divided up into teams of two people on a team. Although we couldn't speak Russia, we communicated with the people in the market place that God loves them and wants them to read His Word. Stu and I gave out all the Bibles we had with us, in a short time.

That afternoon, after lunch, we visited another orphanage. Like the first one we visited in a personal way, then they presented a program with singing and dancing. Two girls gave an instrumental presentation, and then Stu charmed them with his singing. After the program, the children mobbed him for his autograph.

The following day was Victory Day for the Russians. They fervently celebrate the victory over Nazi Germany on May 9, 1945. Parades are held all over Russia. Red Square would have a military parade with tanks and regiments of marching soldiers.

A Trip Realized

Brother Harold said, "Today, at noon, we've being invited to a banquet with the honored Russian soldiers who fought in World War II. These men are retired generals and leaders. They are retired at a special assisted living place here in Kaluga."

We dressed in our best attire for the banquet. The banquet was held in a large spacious room with a long twenty-foot table. The retired Russian military men were in their seventies and eighties. A few were in their early nineties.

The food was delicious. After the meal, the waiters brought in the glasses for vodka. We filled our glasses with coke and heartily lifted them in toast after toast.

I was amazed at how much those old soldiers could drink. Surely their blood pressure went amuck. When we had finished eating, Stu brought several songs. The old soldiers enjoyed his singing.

One of the retired men in the group was formerly the KGB Director for East Germany. He especially liked Stu's singing and had Stu sit beside him. They carried on conversation in his broken English and through an interpreter.

Stu shared the Good News of Jesus with him and the former KGB Leader opened his heart to receive Jesus and His promise of eternal life. We all rejoiced along with the angels in glory!

One of the highlights of the trip was our visit to Chief Justice Gulnara Belenkaya's home. Harold had met Judge Gulnara on a previous trip. He had given her a Gospel of John, even though she had boasted to him that she was an atheist. Harold replied to her boast prophetically, "Judge, you will come to know Jesus Christ in your heart and life as Lord and Savior."

Judge Gulnara and her daughter were almost killed in a car accident. She recovered in a most miraculous way. Through that experience, and the witness of the Gospel through Brother Harold, the Judge came to confess Jesus as Lord and Savior. Judge Gulnara now gives out Bibles to those who come before her in court.

Judge Gulnara received us graciously. Her daughters and friends served us tea and sweet cakes. After a time of visiting, the Judge asked Harold to lead in a worship service. He led in a short service, and then he asked the Judge to give her testimony.

A Trip Realized

On the next to the last day in Kaluga, we went back to the market and finished handing out the four thousand Bibles and other literature. Then we went back to the hotel to pack up for our return trip the next day.

When we arrived in Moscow the next day, we stopped at McDonalds to get a Big Mac. Wow! Was it ever good! Then we checked in the Novatel near the airport for our last night in Russia.

That afternoon, we boarded the trams to go downtown to do souvenir shopping. I was fascinated with the fake Rolex watches that you could buy for a few dollars. They make great souvenirs, so I bought a number of them for family and friends.

But the most important thing we took out of Russia was the memories of our Christian friends and the experiences that we shared with them.

Brother Harold: A Channel of Blessing

One day as Harold drove downtown in Clarksville, part of his car muffler dropped down and drug on the pavement. Seeing a muffler repair shop, he pulled in and inquired about the repair of his muffler. The workshop foreman said, "Go sit in the waiting room and we'll call you when your muffler is repaired and ready."

While waiting in the room, a man came in needing muffler repairs on an old Cadillac. While waiting he asked Harold, "What kind of work do you do?"

Harold replied, "I'm a missionary. I just got back from Russia a few days ago."

The man said, "Wonderful! Today is your day. I'm the marketing manager of a tile company, and I have hundreds of truck loads of tile that I want to give away and you're the man who can give it away to churches, missionaries and orphanages."

Harold asked, "Where's your factory located?"

"Here's my card with the address. Come down on Monday morning and I'll show you what we have to give away."

Monday morning Harold drove to the address on the card. The marketing manager met him and showed him around the factory. Harold said, "I could hardly believe what I saw. The stacks of tile ran about a half-mile. There were hundreds of tractor trailer loads of tile to be given away, and he wanted me to give it away."

Through the years, Harold had been a conduit to give things away to others. But when he tried to give away the tile, no one seemed to believe him. Harold said to a friend, "Hundreds of tractor trailer loads of tile were for anyone who wanted them and I couldn't give the tile away. I called friends, pastors, missionaries and Christian organizations, but they didn't believe the tile was free."

Some weeks later, the marketing manager met with Harold. "Harold" he said, "I'm gonna shut down the program of giving away the tile. Nothing is moving."

"Sir, give me another two months, would you?"

"Okay, but I want to see the tile moving out. It needs to be given away."

Then the break came: Early one Saturday morning the phone rang at Harold's house. "Hello, is this Harold Witmer? The voice said, "I'm Bill Gothard. I hear you have some tile to give away. May I have a truck load?"

"Yes sir, you can have a truck load."

Encouraged by the response, Bill Gothard then said, "Brother Harold, can I have two truck loads?"

"Brother," Harold said, "you can have as many truck loads as you want."

That telephone conversation was the beginning of a relationship between Bill Gothard and Brother Harold that still exists until today. Harold shipped out dozens of tractor-trailer loads of tile to Bill Gothard's training centers and orphanages all over the world.

Bill Gothard publicized the tile give-away program in his seminars, and Harold's telephone began ringing. The tile began to move big time.

In looking back over the tile give-away program, Harold summed up the experience with a spiritual lesson: "When God gets ready to do something, be prepared for He may want to use you. Your life and situation can change in a moment of time. Be open and ready for God to use you, at any time, to carry out His will and purpose."

Brother Harold: A Channel of Blessing

Dave called Harold from a Chicago mission. "Brother Harold can you use a dish washer? I mean a large dish washer that's worth thousands of dollars."

"Dave, I don't have any use for it, but I'll take it and give it away for you."

At that very time, unbeknown to Brother Harold, a group of staff members in the Bill Gothard Center in Chicago were praying for a large dishwasher. Bill Gothard, himself, happened to drop by. He challenged the group, "Why don't you fast and pray?"

Later on one of Bill Gothard's staff members called Brother Harold. "Do you happen to have a large dishwasher?"

"Yeah, I do," Brother Harold said.

"How much do you want for it?"

"Nothing. You just pay the expenses to get it there."

That's the way Harold operates. He's an open vessel to allow God to channel material and spiritual blessings through him to others.

Giving the Gospel to the Golfers

Brother Harold Witmer was the most unlikely person to become friends with Bobby Greenwood, Jack Wall and other PGA golfers. He was not a golfer, nor the son of a golfer. As a matter of fact, he had never played a round of golf in his life.

God walked Brother Harold into the lives of these pro golfers, and they will always be grateful for that happening.

It's always amazing how God works through His children to get His message to others.

One day Brother Harold got a call from Tony Romeo, Baptist Student Union Director at Kentucky Western University. At one time Tony played tight end for the Dallas Texans, and later on for the Boston Patriots, in the American Football league.

Tony said, "Brother Harold, I just came back from holding a revival in upstate New York. A golf pro by the name of Jack Wall came forward professing Christ Jesus as Lord and Savior. He needs to be followed up. He's transferring to a golf course in Hopkinsville, Kentucky where he'll be the head pro there. Would you go visit him and encourage him in the Lord?"

"Sure Tony, I'll be glad too. I know where the golf course is located."

Harold and Faye visited Jack, his wife Linda, and daughter Lisa. Jack and his family were excited about the visit and responded warmly. They traded information about their families, and Jack told about his new job as golf pro at the Hopkinsville Country club.

Harold changed the conversation to get to the purpose of their visit. "Jack, Linda and Lisa, we'll be praying for you as you get located here. Remember, God has a put you in this place, at this time, for a purpose. We'll be praying that God's will be done in your lives."

After praying together with the family, Faye took Linda's hand. "Linda, you must visit us in Clarksville. We want to get to know you better."

The Wall family became close friends with Harold and Faye. After several months, they moved next door to the Witmers. Harold and Faye were a great encouragement to them in their Christian walk.

Later on Jack Wall organized the Bench craft Golf Company and set the company up on Church Street in

Nashville. During the early beginning of the company, Jack met Bobby Greenwood, a PGA member from Cookeville, Tennessee. He was impressed with Bobby's swing, and he had every reason to be impressed.

Bobby Greenwood was twice ranked in the Top Ten Amateurs in the US both by *Gold Magazine* and *Golf Digest.* He was three times NCAA All American at North Texas State University and was inducted in their Sports Hall of Fame in 2002. He was inducted into the Tennessee Golf Hall of Fame in 2007. In October 2007, he was inducted into the Riverside Military Academy Centennial All-Sports Hall of Fame in Gainesville, Georgia.

Bobby Greenwood was one of the few amateur golfers to beat Jack Nicklaus. As a twenty-four old, he beat Nicklaus at the Colonial in Memphis in a close and memorable match. Greenwood went on to turn pro and to play for seven years on the PGA Tour.

Jack Wall offered Bobby twenty-five percent of his company, if he would come and teach at Bench Craft one day a week. Bobby agreed, so he would drive to Nashville, spend the night at the company and be ready to teach the next morning.

Giving the Gospel to the Golfers

One day Harold accompanied Jack Wall to Nashville to see how his company operated. While there, he met Bobby Greenwood. Bobby and Harold immediately hit it off.

Bobby spoke of Brother Harold and his sharing with one another: "We would leave the hustle and bustle of the company and go out in the alley by the dumpster and talk. One of my few talents is to identify greatness in people. I was immediately intrigued by the honest sincerity of Brother Harold Witmer. I could truly tell that he loved the Lord. But, at that time, I had no idea of the magnitude of that love. He was completely sold out to Jesus."

Jack and Bobby began to take Harold to their golf clinics in the Bahamas and other places. Harold became their official Golf Chaplain for Bench craft Golf Company.

Some of the golf pros invited Harold to preach in their churches. He did and word spread. Others wanted him to share in their home churches. Harold preached the sunrise service on the beach in the Bahamas. Bobby spoke of this service: "It was great! Many people heard about the saving power of Jesus Christ."

Brother Harold

Wherever Brother Harold went with Jack and Bobby, he always looked for opportunities to share the Gospel. Bobby and Jack invited Harold to go with them for that very purpose. They wanted him to share Jesus with their golfing friends.

Harold remembered those exciting days: "It was a great opportunity in my life to meet with these golf pros and to share with them the powerful message of the new birth. Today we are still friends with several of them as we continue in the Lord's work."

During the time spent with Bobby and Jack, Harold served as a mentor to them. Bobby spoke of Brother Harold as a mentor: "Through the years and travels together, I have learned how to love God and to obey His commandments. I am a better Christian man because of being with Brother Harold Witmer."

Bobby described an incredible happening that took place at the Senior PGA Championship held at Laurel Valley Country Club at Ligonier, Pennsylvania: "I played a practice round with the great Arnold Palmer and after the round we went into the luxurious clubhouse to have lunch. We were eating with the world leaders in the golf world. Brother Harold was just resting in the Lord and relaxing. After lunch we made our way through the large crowd of spectators on our way to the practice range. I brought Brother Harold through the ropes and he began talking with several golf pros, as I continued to hit range balls."

Then Bobby described this unforgettable scene: "The next thing I knew, a hush fell over the crowd. Brother Harold had a circle of golf pros around him kneeling in prayer. Later I learned that Chi Chi Rodriguez had requested that Brother Harold pray for him about a special need in his life."

Harold became life long friends with Chi Chi Rodriguez and several other golf pros.

Harold has nothing but fond memories of his "fun" time with the golf pros. He still communicates with several of them. Their lives were blessed and enriched by a man who knows nothing about golf, but he knows a lot about eternal life and the pathway to our Savior Jesus Christ.

Dealing with Life After a Massive Heart Attack

Not many people make it to the Emergency Room with the kind of massive heart attack that Brother Harold suffered in September 2004.

Brother Harold was working in his office with his daughter, Melanie, when sweat starting pouring from his forehead due to severe pain across his chest. Harold knew something was wrong. He said to Melanie, "I'm taking you home."

"Are you all right Dad?"

"Yeah, I'm going to drop you off at the house and I'm going somewhere."

Harold planned to drive to the VA Hospital in Nashville, fifty miles away. When he passed Memorial Hospital, upon leaving Clarksville, the pain was so severe that he knew he wouldn't make it to Nashville, so he wheeled into the parking lot of Memorial Hospital.

He went into the Emergency Entrance and fell across the counter and said, "I need help." A nurse came out and said, "My goodness, this man is having a heart attack."

Dealing with Life After a Massive Heart Attack

She called for a wheel chair and took him immediately into the emergency room. Several doctors came and gave him some nitroglycerin and hooked him to the IV.

Harold was barely able to breathe. Linda Durwachter, who worked in the ER, asked for Faye's phone number and called her. She told Faye, "Harold has had a heart attack and you need to come immediately. He's in bad shape."

Harold was in too much trauma to be highlighted to Vanderbilt Hospital in Nashville. He seemed to have only minutes to live. Linda called Dr. Bill Corley who was out of town that day with Clark, Linda's husband, and immediately got a prayer chain in motion.

Faye picked up their grandson, Joseph, at a friend's house, and they raced to the hospital in record time.

After the prayer chain went into action, Brother Harold's stats began to change dramatically. When the word got out, a number of doctors came by to witness the remarkable change in Harold's condition.

Brother Harold was admitted to Critical Care. The next day he was tested to see the extent of the damage to his heart. His heart had only fifteen per cent function left. He needed bypass surgery in order to give him any time at all. He was taken by ambulance to Vanderbilt Hospital where he had surgery a few days later.

Camping out in the Critical Care Waiting Room is an experience that one can hardly ever forget. Faye and Melanie waited, along with a number of other families, for a word about their loved ones. Most all of the loved ones were in critical condition.

When Faye looked at the tense faces of the waiting families, her heart went out to them. She thought: *Not only are they waiting to see if their loved ones are going to make it, they will have also heavy medical expenses. Some of the families are just trying to deal with day-to-day expenses.*

Faye and Melanie were thankful to see that several churches came with sandwiches and other snack foods during their time in Critical Care. They praised the Lord for this thoughtful ministry carried out in the Name of Christ.

A few hours before Harold's surgery, he called for Faye to come to his bedside. He said, "Faye, I don't feel good about this surgery."

Dealing with Life After a Massive Heart Attack

Brother Harold then gave Faye orders about how to handle his business and funeral arrangements. After they had prayer together, Brother Harold was taken for prepping. They found out later that while waiting his turn for the surgery, his heart did stop and the medical team had to take him in early in order to save his life.

Brother Harold's heart was severely damaged, so the surgery took longer than most usual. He was unable to breathe without machines. On the third day, his stats were up high enough to move him from the recovery room to a private room.

Brother Harold was so sick that he was hardly able to move in the bed. After a while a nurse came in and said to him, "Mr. Witmer, you're going to have to walk."

Brother Harold answered with a weak voice, "I can't even roll over in bed, much less walk."

The nurse came back later that afternoon. She said, "Mr. Witmer, we can't make you walk."

"What will happen if I don't walk?"

She said, "If you can't and won't walk, they'll move you to a nursing home, and you will have to recover there."

Upon hearing this, Brother Harold said, "I'm ready to walk right now."

Faye looked at the nurse, smiled and said, "He means it."

The next day Brother Harold asked the same nurse, "What must I do to get released to go home?"

"You have to walk around this entire hallway."

"Tomorrow," Brother Harold said, "I'll run around this hallway."

The following day, Brother Harold did not run around the hallway, but he did walk around it, however, at a very slow pace.

After returning home, Harold still experienced a lot of pain; but each day he got stronger. One day he felt strong enough to go to his office for a few minutes. After several days, he went for a longer period of time.

Life has changed drastically for Harold Witmer. No more charging through life full steam each day; he has adapted to a new life style. There would be no more mission trips to Russia. He can only travel short distances.

One day Brother Harold asked Faye, "Why did I have to go through all this when God could have healed me instantly?"

She replied, "Yes, God could have healed you instantly, but maybe you were so busy that you didn't take time to hear Him speak to you."

Brother Harold has listened to the voice of God in a new and exciting way. He has experienced the tremendous moving of the Holy Spirit in his life. God gave him a message to give to his friends: "That which is born of the flesh is flesh and that which is born of the Spirit is Spirit." (John 3)

The Lord impressed Harold to have an "office ministry" where the Lord would send people from all over the world to his office to receive his message and ministry.

That's exactly what has happened. On any given day, Brother Harold's office has people from all walks of life and from all places.

After Brother Harold's surgery, he was told that he would have a year and a half to live. They said that his heart would never improve. It has been almost nine years and after his most recent examination, he was told that he now has thirty-five percent of his heart's function. That's a great difference from fifteen percent, isn't it? Praise the Lord!

Brother Harold: Servant of the Lord

Who is Brother Harold Witmer? What kind of a man is he? How does he live day by day?

First of all, Brother Harold is a servant of Jesus Christ. He is concerned about advancing the Kingdom of Christ. Whenever he can, wherever he goes, whatever he does, he has in mind to honor Jesus and to advance His cause.

He gives attention to all races and classes of society without any bias. Brother Charles, a saxophone player, who's a faithful servant in Community Church and in Harold's office, said, "Brother Harold is always here for those who need help. He's my man. He's my brother in the Lord."

Robert is another friend of Brother Harold. He can be seen in Brother Harold's office at almost any time of the day. Robert spent so much time in the city jail that they wanted him to pay rent. One day, when he was out of jail, he wandered into Brother Harold's office. Brother Harold led him to experience God's forgiveness and a new life in Jesus.

158

Brother Harold: Servant of the Lord

Robert attends the Community church. Harold's office is sort of his home. He's there to run errands or to do what needs to be done. He said, "When Brother Harold comes into the office, he brings hamburgers, donuts, pizzas and other snacks for those of us who're short on money. Anybody can come in and eat, if they want too. Every day we'll have people come in, eat, and quietly go out. If they want to talk, okay, and if they don't, that's okay too."

Robert continued, "Brother Harold has made it possible for me to have a second chance in life. Here, I'm treated with respect, and I know that Brother Harold and his friends care for me. I'm blessed."

Brother Harold is a gentle man. He's soft-spoken and never intimidating. When the situation calls for it, he can be bold and tough. After all, Brother Harold is the one who took Bibles to Russia shortly after the wall came down. He went straight up to the gate of the Russian military base and talked and motioned enough to get into the base. After handing out all of the Bibles, he and his group were told to leave.

Brother Harold is a caring husband, father and grandfather. He tenderly cares for Faye and always treats her with the greatest respect. He gives attention to her input and counsel.

His children love and respect him. They'll tell you that he has always loved and cared for them, but he was never a pushover. He was tough with them when the time called for him to be tough.

Ask his grandchildren. They will tell you that granddad is no wimp. When they're staying at his house, they abide by the household rules. He's tough, but he's a softie in many ways. He'll slip them money when needed and provide for other teenage needs.

Those who know Brother Harold will tell you that he's a giver. Jim Labrec, a friend, said, "Brother Harold will give away everything that he has."

Harold, himself, said, "I want to be a conduit, a channel and give away everything that God gives to me. I don't care anything about money or material things for myself. I want to be God's channel to get these things to people who need them. God has impressed me to be a total giver."

Brother Harold continued to say, "You know, you can't out give God. One day the funds were low. We didn't know how we were going to keep operating with our many programs. Then a man walks into my office and hands me a check. I thanked him and put the check on top of my desk. I thought that the check would be for fifty or maybe a hundred dollars. When the man left my office, I picked up the check. I almost fell out of my chair. The check was for ten thousand dollars!"

Brother Harold strongly believes that God has called him to give away all that God gives to him. He said, "I don't believe that everybody is called to give away all that God has given to them, but I believe that God has called me to be a conduit to pass on what the Lord has given to me to others.

Christian Partners is the organization that Brother Harold felt led to form several years ago. It sponsors dozens of missionaries and mission groups throughout the world. It sponsors six plus orphanages in Russian plus a 250-acre farm that has a facility to address the needs of addicts of alcohol and drugs. It is the organization that has worked with Pastor Gregory to start thirty new churches in the Kaluga area.

Christian Partners expresses Brother Harold's desire to share the Gospel with the world. He is a witness, both through his organizations and on a personal basis.

He's generous in helping others, but he uses that as a door to enter with the Good News of Christ.

Brother Harold began leading others to the Savior just after he was saved, and he has continued on to this day.

Some day in heaven, hundreds of people will be coming up to Brother Harold and saying, "Thank you, Brother Harold, thank you. Thank you for sharing Jesus and eternal life with me."

The great Methodist evangelist and leader, John Wesley, who was a very generous person, said, "I live simply that I might give more."

That's describes Brother Harold and Faye. They live simple and unassuming lives that they might give more to others. Brother Harold drives an old model car of whatever kind is given to him. He and Faye live in a modest house that they have lived in for the past thirty-five years.

They are like the older black lady who said, "I wear the world like a loose garment"

They do wear the world like a loose garment, for they know that the world is passing away and only those who do the will of God will live forever.

Brother Harold: Servant of the Lord

Brother Harold is, not only a giver, he's a disciple maker-maker. He never gives up on anyone. He takes a person for what they are, where they are, and he tries to lead them to experience all that Christ has for them. He waits on a disciple, or a potential disciple, laughs with them, cries with them, feeds them, rejoices with them and is always leading them toward a higher and godly goal.

Many disciples have no time, or take no time to listen and learn from others. They are busy, busy and are chasing after so many pleasures and pursuits in life that they do not want to sit at the feet of Jesus to learn the meaning of life.

Brother Harold knows this group, and he waits until the storms of life hits them and jars them awake. Only then do they come to him and are willing to listen and learn.

The late Dr. Bill Corley spoke about Harold as a disciple maker: "Brother Harold is a great listener; however, to be around him you would think the opposite. He has the uncanny ability to talk and listen at the same time. Just when you think that he could not have possibly heard what you were saying, he will hit you with a simple question that confounds the wise."

Brother Harold

Dan Calderon, owner and manager of WCKV-TV in Clarksville gives his perspective of Brother Harold as a servant of the Lord: "I have known Brother Harold Witmer for about a dozen years and I am never surprised to see or hear about how God has used him and his ministries to fulfill a need."

"When I started the small broadcast TV station in Clarksville, several people suggested I meet with Brother Harold to learn about his Christian ministry. It was operating at the time out of the old mill and to be quite frank, the first impression was, well to put it kindly, in the South they say, 'bless your heart.' Brother Harold was always dressed in simple attire and the surrounding was dirty, smelled of fungus, and on one occasion I even saw a mouse cut across the floor within three feet of where I sat. I actually was concerned about Brother Harold's health being in that place all the time and prayed that he would find a better location."

"The reason I kept coming back was the sweet spirit of the Lord that was always present. I loved hearing the stories of how God worked out this or that, small and large, simple and difficult. Some people talk about their faith, but Brother Harold just humbly does it."

One of the highest honors that can be given to Brother Harold is to simply call him "a servant of Jesus Christ."

Rise Up and Call Her Blessed

While Brother Harold was off on crusades, on mission trips to Russia or across town on business, Faye has kept the home fires burning. She has reared the children, taught Sunday School, played the piano and organ for the church.

Faye is a Magna Cum Laude graduate of Northwestern Music Conservatory. She could have used her musical talents to pursue a music career, but she has, for the past fifty years, used her God-given talent to play for the local churches, for crusades and for social events. She has never received any remuneration for her services.

Dr Bill Corley called Faye "One of the greatest musicians in all of Christendom."

On top of everything else that Faye did, she decided to go into the real estate business. Typical of Faye, she studied and prepared herself to be the best agent possible. Her real estate business has flourished, and she has become one of the most well reputed agents in Clarksville.

But more than all of these talents and successful activities, Faye is a homemaker, a loving wife, mother and grandmother.

Although she is a devoted wife and mother, she has taken time to go on the first Russian trip with Harold, accompanied the team on evangelistic tours, directed choirs, played the organ and piano and taught Sunday School each week.

Several years ago Faye suffered a terrible blot clot in her leg, and later a stroke. Her faith never wavered as she went through rehabilitation, and she has fully recovered. She has adjusted her life by eating healthier kinds of food and is now going full speed in her ministry and work.

Faye had perfect peace in the Lord to keep His promise of eternal life when she buried both her father and mother. She was at Harold's side when he suffered a massive heart attack and hovered at death's door for several days. Faye looked at a million dollars worth of hospital bills and trusted the Lord to help her in that overwhelming debt. Jesus never disappoints!

God's people are not immune from accidents, even though they are often not at fault. Such was the case of Faye when a young man on a motorcycle swerved and crashed into her car on the parkway. She prayed as she stood over him and watched him die. She also reached out to the Lord in praying faith for her grandson who nearly died of leukemia.

Through it all, Faye has never quit trusting Jesus. She knows the meaning of the song *Through It All*:

Through it all, through it all,

I've learned to trust in Jesus, I've learned to trust in God.

Through it all I've learned to depend upon His Word.

Faye did all these things and is doing them now by faith, a faith that is a kindred faith with Brother Harold's. It's a faith that believes Jesus keeps His promises.

A Faith That Deals with Stress

A common theme from those who have spent time with Brother Harold is that he is able to deal with the most stressful situations by turning these challenges over to the Lord. When confronted with a problem or a situation where things have gone wrong or have not worked out according to schedule, Brother Harold demonstrates a faith that faces these problems without getting stressed out.

Bill Harrison went to Russia with Brother Harold in 1998. He said, "I'd rather go to Russia with Harold than anyone else. He never gets uptight. Watching Harold wait on the Lord as numerous obstacles arose taught me to let go and let God take over."

Hubert White made eight trips to Russia with Brother Harold. He said, "We arrived late in the Netherlands and had to run to catch our flight to Moscow. Nothing seemed to bother Brother Harold. "

They made it to Moscow okay, but because of the rush to catch the flight, their baggage did not arrive with them. It presented a problem, because all of the Bibles and supplies were in their luggage. After flying for twenty-four hours, it was difficult to take that kind of disappointment.

They were in a bind. Brother Harold and Hubert were to catch a bus to Ludinova where they had planned a weeklong ministry. The bus was to leave at nine o'clock for a nine-hour trip. Brother Harold said, "We can't leave without our Bibles and other supplies. Without them our trip will be a failure."

The ticket agent said, "An Aeroflot flight is coming in at six o'clock, but it's unlikely that your baggage will be on it. You used another airline."

They went to the hotel near the airport and met with their interpreter. Brother Harold said to Hubert, "There's no way we can get on that bus without our Bibles and supplies."

"Hubert," Brother Harold said, "We've got to take this to the Lord."

He prayed, "Lord, we've traveled to the other side of the world to tell these people about You, and to bring them gifts from the folks back home. Now it appears that we're going to have to go back home and tell them that the gifts were lost and we were not able to complete our mission. Hubert and I have come to Moscow just like You told us to do, and Lord It's up to You to get the supplies to us. Please do it, Lord, in Jesus name. Amen."

Hubert said, "The situation didn't look good. Although it was highly unlikely that Aeroflot would have our five pieces of luggage, we sent the interpreter back to the airport to check. All five pieces of our luggage were on that flight! This had to be the hand of God. Praise His name!"

On the 1998 trip to Russia, some of the team members were concerned whether their luggage would make it on time, or even make it. The duffel bags had all of the Bibles, Christian literature and gifts for the children in six orphanages. No wonder the team members were worried.

Brother Harold put things in perspective for the team. He said, "Listen, we did all that we were supposed to do. We took the luggage to the airport; God will do the rest."

God did do the rest. The team's entire luggage arrived, and on time.

Community Church sponsored a team of teen-agers to go on a mission trip to Honduras., but they didn't have enough funds. Pastor Harold challenged the congregation to give the needed ten thousand dollars. The offering plates were passed around twice, but only five thousand was received.

Brother Harold was not perplexed about not getting enough money from the offering. One of the church elders came by after the service and said, "We didn't get the needed money, did we?"

Brother Harold replied, "No, we didn't, but the money will come in. These young people want to carry the Gospel to Honduras and the Lord will provide what's needed."

That week a man came by the office and handed Brother Harold a check that covered the needs of the team. The check brought the total up to ten thousand dollars.

Coming back from the 1998 trip to Russia, Hubert White describes a frustrating experience for the team: "When we arrived at the United Airlines counter, we found that Northwest Airlines had not done a very good job of confirming our seats, so we had another delay. As we were about to board the flight, it was postponed because of a severe storm. Things were really getting a little frustrating for the team."

Hubert spoke of Brother Harold's response to the frustrating situation: "Again nothing seems to bother Brother Harold. He truly has the faith of a child when it comes to walking with God. We were told that we could get on the flight to St. Louis. I was surprised to see that the plane was a small twin-engine prop job. I got uptight about that. Brother Harold laughed and said to me, 'the engine runs with rubber bands.' That helped me a little…but not much."

Brother Harold's relaxed, trusting demeanor relaxes others and helps them to trust the situation to the Lord's hands. He knows, like the Psalmist that "our time is in His hands." (Psalms31:15)

Pastor Harold

The Lord had always given Brother Harold leadership and guidance in the local church. He was one of the guiding forces in visualizing and organizing the Community Church. After the church was organized, he became one of the first elders.

Later on, Brother Harold became the Mission's Director of the church. He and Dr. Bill Corley, the pastor, shared the same vision that wanted the congregation to give 50% to missions and to operate on 50%. Brother Harold had the responsibility of building home and foreign missions under Dr. Corley's leadership.

The mission project that was the closest to Brother Harold's heart, and the largest mission project, was the Kaluga, Russia Project. The Berlin Wall had just come down and there was a lot of freedom in Russia, at this time, to share the Gospel of Jesus Christ.

The Kaluga Project grew rapidly and today is one of the largest Protestant Church Movements in Russia.

After ten years of leading teams into Russia and handling all of the annual tours, Brother Harold suffered a massive heart attack. Now, he is limited to local ministry in Clarksville.

Although Brother Harold cannot travel as he did before, he visualized a ministry of ministering to those that the Lord sends to him day by day. He's in his office on Main Street day by day and it's amazing to see the people who come by to meet and talk with him. Missionaries, preachers and people from all walks of life drop by to talk and pray with him.

At this time, Brother Harold's son, Dr. Steve Witmer, has taken the mantle of leadership of the Kaluga Project.

It was during the time of Brother Harold's recovery that Dr. Corley became very ill. He said to Brother Harold, "I want you to fill in and do some preaching."

When Dr. Corley's condition worsened, he called Brother Harold to his bedside and said, "I want you to pastor the church."

Brother Harold was taken by surprise. He replied, "Brother Bill, I don't think I can do it."

"Yes, you can do it. I've watched you. You can make tough decisions which you will have to do as pastor."

When Dr. Corley was in his last hours on earth, he called in the elders of Community Church. He told them, "I want Brother Harold Witmer to take my place as pastor of Community Church. He'll be faithful in leading the church."

The elders agreed with Dr. Corley's request and when he passed away, Brother Harold became the pastor.

Brother Harold recently spoke about his responsibility as pastor: "I would never have believed that the pastorate was such a tough and awesome responsibility. From the nursery to the senior citizens and everything in between ends up on the desk of the pastor."

Dr. Freeman, pastor of the First Baptist Church in Clarksville, asked Brother Harold, "How are things going at the church?"

"Dr. Freeman, I've got to do a lot of repenting. I had no idea what the pastor goes through day by day. I was harder on Dr. Corley than I should have been."

Recently, Brother Harold summarized Community Church's progress: "Today the church has reached its vision of giving 50% to missions and have a strong elder and deacon board who are learning to disciple others."

A Son's Testimony

"It has been said that if you want to know something about a man, just ask his family. As a son of Brother Harold, these are the things I want to say about my father."

Brother's Harold's son, Steven, made the enclosed statements to sum up his love for his father. The commentary remarks are the author's:

"Dad is a man of true faith. He believes that God is who He says He is, and can do what He says He can do."

Brother Harold's transparent faith is and has been an inspiration to many people. While leading teams to Russia over a period of ten years, the team members had the opportunity to see Brother Harold's faith in action. They saw his faith whether waiting for their missing baggage or trying to get into a Russian military base.

Many times the Board of the Youth Challenge Center witnessed Brother Harold's faith in waiting for the Lord to meet the physical needs for the very next day.

"He is a man of action. While most men talk about things they want to do, Dad jumps in and does it."

While others were talking about taking Bibles into Russia, Brother Harold took Bibles into Russia. While others were talking about what should be done about the youth in Clarksville, Brother Harold worked together with Jim Yeatts to organize Youth Challenge.

"Dad is a man of vision. He asks God what He wants to do, so God shows him."

Brother Harold has a deep, personal relationship with God. The Lord led him to organize Youth Challenge, and he did it. The Lord laid it upon his heart to take Bibles to Russia, and he did it. He felt led to organize the first interdenominational church in Clarksville, and he did it by working together with men who shared a similar vision.

"He is a man of the Word. Dad believes God's Word is exactly that…God's Word."

Brother Harold's love and respect for God's Word is shown by his desire to read, to study, to teach and to preach the Word of Life anywhere, to anyone who will listen.

"Dad is a man of the Gospel. He has lived a life committed to getting out this message—Jesus Saves!

Whether on the streets of York, Pennsylvania, Clarksville, Tennessee, or Kaluga, Russia, Brother Harold has been diligent in sharing the Good News of Jesus Christ with others.

"Dad is a man of the people. He loves everyone because all are loved by God."

Come and visit in Brother Harold's downtown office, and you will see the rich and the poor and people of all races come into His office. They come because they know they will be received with the love of Jesus. They come because they feel welcome.

"Dad is a man of the church. He believes the church is the Bride of Christ and that God works through the local church to accomplish His will."

From the time of his salvation to the present time, Brother Harold has worked in and through the local church. He attends pastor's meetings, and is in almost daily contact with pastors, Church leaders and members from different denominations.

"Dad is a man of faithfulness. He has remained committed to God and my mother for all these years."

One of the characteristics our Lord stressed in the New Testament is faithfulness. Brother Harold has been found faithful in his commitment to the Lord Jesus and to his wife, Faye. While others have dropped out in the race of life, or given up, Brother Harold has kept on course for Jesus. His faithfulness has been a witness to his family and friends.

"Dad is a man of generosity. He has lived to bless others. Most people could never repay him for all he has done for them, including me, his son."

People who know Brother Harold know that he gives away about everything that is given to him. He told a friend recently, "I want to give away everything that God gives to me." His generosity has blessed the world.

A personal word from Steven, to his dad, Brother Harold:
"Thanks Dad for being the great man that you are. I love you and may the Kingdom of God continue to be expanded through your love and efforts to serve Christ. That would be your wish, that this book would bring God honor and that through reading it, people would be saved as they see what God can do through a simple man who truly believes and is committed to following his Savior and Lord, Jesus Christ."
Your Son,   Steve

Brother Harold

Barbara Corley's Testimony

When Harold Witmer was obedient to the Lord, and walked into my husband's office at First Christian Church, Bill Corley's life was changed forever, and so was mine. Bill had always believed every word in the Bible to be true. He had preached the truth since he was seventeen years-old, but he had never before known the security of salvation.

When Harold asked Bill to quote John 3:16, he immediately quoted it. Then Harold asked him to quote it again, this time inserting the name Bill where "world" was before. He had never done that and he was immediately transformed. He became so excited talking about Jesus that he shouted and shared Jesus with everyone that he met.

Bill and Harold became inseparable companions. The more Bill got "turned on," the more I got "turned off." I did not like this man, Harold Witmer, at all. Maybe I was jealous of his time with Bill, or maybe I resented the joy these men possessed. I knew that Harold Witmer was one of my least favorite people.

I could write a book about the relationship of these two men but time does not permit. After a couple of years, Bill became dissatisfied at the church. Brother Harold, Elder Davis Potts and a few others approached him about starting another church. God moved in that situation and the Community church came into existence. Bill became the pastor.

The church faced many challenged, but fulfilled its purpose to win the lost. Harold led out in evangelism and missions. The spirit of love and oneness prevailed, and yes, I had come around to care for Brother Harold.

Bill and Harold held numerous evangelistic meetings together, and when one had a need, the other one was there to help meet the need.

When Bill became ill, he spent hours in prayer. He knew that he would have to make some major decisions about the church and its ministry. When the time came for him to leave for the hospital, he knew decision time had arrived. Harold was at the house that morning, as were a few others. Just before Bill went out the door, he looked at Harold and said, "Harold, you're in charge until I come back."

Bill did not say it just once, he repeated it several times. He looked at me and said, "Barbara, did you hear me? Harold is to be in charge until I return."

Bill was very emphatic about Harold being in charge. I do believe, however, that he thought he would be back.

As Bill's illness progressed, he sank quickly. One day he told me that he had two regrets. The first was that he had not completed Harold's book. The other was that he would not see the Fellowship Hall built. He thought that the church, and especially the young people, really needed that facility.

One morning, at the hospital, he said, "Barbara, I want Harold and Davis. I want them now, as soon as they can get here."

He was issuing orders, even though he was dying; and he witnessed until his last breath. The two men came, as soon as they were contacted. When they arrived, he said he wanted everyone out of the room but the nurse, who was required to be in the room, and the two men.

How blessed was Christy, the nurse, who remained in the room. She said, "I felt like I was observing a super-natural mountain top experience. A bright glow entered the room like nothing I've ever seen before. The presence of the Lord was in that place."

I do not know what Bill said to Harold and Davis Potts, and I never asked him. This was a very private time with these three men who dearly loved one another and were closer than brothers.

I was aware that Bill knew that he was dying and

time was running out. He repeated again that he wanted Harold to take his place, as pastor of the church.

A short time later, Bill Corley was escorted, by the angels in glory, from his earthly body to the portals of glory to be in the presence of his Lord and Savior, Jesus. To Jesus be glory and honor forever and ever. Amen

**Testimony written by Yvonne Glasman,
Dino's widow.**

Dino Glasman, founder and director of College to World Ministry, loved his interaction with the APSU students and the opportunity to minister to them. APSU, Austin Peay State University, is a 4-year public, masters level university, offering over 56 majors and 63 different concentrations with the primary campus snuggled in downtown Clarksville. It is named after former Tennessee Governor, Austin Peay, and has an enrollment of over 10,000 students.

First and foremost though, Dino loved Jesus Christ. Dino believed that college students of all ages were being challenged to examine their religious beliefs and often philosophical discussions were not limited to the classroom. College to World Ministry was not just about leading students into a growing relationship with Jesus Christ, but it was for those already in a journey with Christ to explore how they could become leaders for Christ when leaving college and moving on into the world with purpose.

It was during the early stages of the ministry that Dino met Joseph Witmer, grandson of Brother Harold. Joe insisted that Dino and Harold meet. That meeting was just one more example of the power of God. It didn't take long to see similarities of these two men. Dino and Harold were

186

committed to being available and obedient to the Lord, not just when it was convenient, but daily. Another similarity was that they both believed that the lost could be found and they both could certainly connect with people. Harold's office was within walking distance (or a bicycle ride) from the APSU campus. Since Dino was in need of office space close to the campus, and as demonstrated throughout Harold's long life, this was just another opportunity to reach out and help another brother in Christ. The office became a home-away-from home for Dino. Compassion and kindness fill the shared office, and Dino was given the privilege to see Harold first hand again witnessing the power of God at work.

Both men not only love the Lord, but they deeply love family. Harold was now active in raising his grandson, Joseph, who holds a special place in his heart. Dino was extremely active in raising his girls as well, and subsequently, would often have his young grandson, Arkell, with him. Arkell and Joseph witnessed first-hand how to be patient, serve others, wait on the Lord, pray without ceasing, and ministry.

Dino and Harold talked about bringing Joseph along in the ministry to get a taste of leadership firsthand. Joseph served as the first and only intern for Christ to the

World Ministry. Because of Joseph's work, C2WM was able to offer more Bible studies and expanded small group interaction. Since these times, Joseph has gone on, married, and focuses on ministry, seeking God's will for his life.

Summer activities and enrollment on a campus often decline, and Harold convinced Dino that Russia was where he needed to focus and be during the summer. So Dino signed up and made several summer trips to Russia, each one packed with excitement and all under God's leading and direction. Several APSU students joined in the journey, including Joseph, Josh Bolin and Richard Yost. Lives were changed for eternity.

The morning of August 25, 2011, Dino rode his new bicycle to the office and then on to campus to help new freshmen and returning students on move-in day. At lunchtime he rode across town to a local bowling alley for a bowling league banquet as the summer season was ending. It was on the way back that Dino was tragically struck by a car and air evacuated to Vanderbilt Hospital in Nashville. Word spread among the students that worked with Dino and at the office. The power of prayer was felt by the family. Dino remained unconscious except to tell his girls that he loved them. Joseph and many others came and prayed over Dino. Harold also came and in his own unique and special way, shared in meeting the immediate needs of the family. Brother Harold offered encouragement, prayer, and love. He was serving, witnessing, and once again simply available to serve the Lord. With hearts breaking, those that loved Dino could find comfort as God's plan for him was being perfected. He went home to be with his Lord and Saviour on Sept. 1st.

Dino considered it a privilege to watch Brother Harold minister to others in so many ways. Harold proved to be a powerful mentor, blessing, and a kindred spirit to Dino. The ministry of both men spreads in ways only the Lord knows. They would want the world to know that we are nothing without God. Dino poured out his life with a passion for the gospel and Harold continues in that same passion for the lost and love for Christ. He'll run the race until the finish line. Praise the Lord!

Brother Harold

10 MAIN STREET

B.J. Peer

The second story office has a view overlooking busy Riverside Dr., the Cumberland River and farm land on the other side. Two large windows face the west allowing views of beautiful sunsets, riverboat activity and cars zooming up and down the busy street. Inside the eclectic office and adorning the entire large back wall are vintage Gospel record album covers collected over the years. Also on the wall are photos of people from past mission trips to Russia, photos of the Servicemen's Center and Boy's Home, as well as colorful posters advertising the Old Time Tent Revival Crusades. These things are not just memorabilia; they attest to Pastor Harold's track record of spreading the Gospel throughout his lifetime.

"Ye know not what a day brings forth," is one of his quotes that reflect the extraordinary happenings that he experiences every day. His steadfastness in the Lord and faith allows the Lord to orchestrate things through and around him.

"Feed my sheep', is a Biblical principle that Pastor Harold takes seriously – literally and spiritually. Often people are waiting for the doors to open at noon for the "lunch program" of pizza, hamburgers, tacos and hotdogs. It becomes a flurry of activity with people coming and going, the phone steadily ringing, along with several separate conversations all going on simultaneously. Some people call or come by to leave a donation, whether it be clothes, a vehicle, household items or a financial gift, because they know that other people come to him with needs, wants and wishes. It is truly amazing to witness on a day to day, week by week and yearly basis how the Lord works through and around Pastor Harold. So many remarkable happenings have occurred at 10 Main Street.

I, too, walked into Pastor Harold's office to talk with him. The Lord had brought his name to my mind on two different occasions as I prayed daily, trying to discern how the Lord wanted me to serve Him to fulfill a distinct calling I had years earlier from the Lord to do mission work. I told Pastor Harold "my story". "I had decided to take early retirement after 19 years of teaching in private, federal and public schools so that I could serve the Lord." Pastor Harold made a phone call to Madison, GA, to speak with Dr. Bill Shade who was the Director of Source of Light Ministry International. He told him to send me down. I served at the SLM headquarters in various departments for one year and then returned to Clarksville. As I shared the discipleship

Bible Studies with people, Pastor Harold saw the vision and importance of getting people grounded in the Word of God. He understood how important discipleship is even though his primary gifting had always been evangelism and leading people to make decisions for the Lord. A Correspondence Discipleship School was chartered with SLM International so that we could use their materials and award certificates for completed course work.

The Lord opened the door one year ago for the School of Light to be able to get the correspondence discipleship courses into the local Montgomery County jail, into the hands of the inmates. It has been very successful with many inmates making decisions for the Lord, rededicating their lives as well as learning how to walk out their faith. It has been so successful that they keep referring other people – family and friends – not just in the jail, but also in the community. One lady was transferred to another jail out of state, where she referred five other women. Those five women referred others and they referred their friends, as well as other family members, too. The Lord is not only growing the individual numbers but He is growing the Outreach as well. Two other schools are being developed as a result in Nashville and Murfreesboro, TN. These schools bring hope and Light into some very dark places.

Pastor Harold often says, "Great battles mean Great Victories." We rely on donations, are faith-based, and offer the discipleship materials to everyone freely as Christ offers His free gift of salvation to all who believe in Him and receive Him. The rewards of the fruit of the labor keep us pressing on toward the mark of the high calling of the Lord, so that some day we may hear Him say, "Well done, good and faithful servant."

Soldier for Jesus and Uncle Sam

Harold sharing Jesus in the Christian Service — Men's Center

Brother Harold:
Director/Admin-
istrator, Christian
Service Men's
Center

Glenn and Jean
Davis Succeeded
Harold and Faye at
the CSMC

Glenn Davis, manager of the Servicemen's Center, his wife, Jean. Davis also is a teacher at Howell School. (Staff Photo by W. J. Souza).

Youth Challenge met a great need
among the youth in Clarksville

Great crowds turned out for the
Youth Challenge Crusades

Brother Harold and Mel Johnson hit
the saw dust trail in the Northern
States with their big tent.

Brother Harold in his
red jacket ready to
leave for Russia

Brother Harold relating to a Russian officer in
East Germany

Pastor Gregori's church in Kaluga, Russia

Harold and team at a banquest
in their honor at Kaluga, Russia

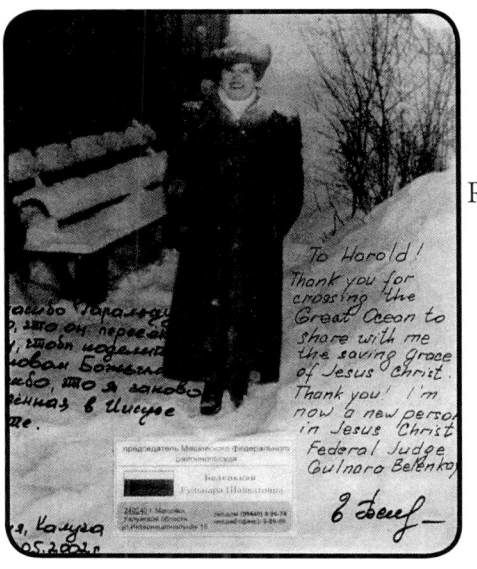

Russian Federal Judge,
Gulnara Belenkay,
trusted Jesus

Harold with Russian orphans

Brother Harold, Hubert White and
Steve Witmer (Harold's son) at an orphanage near Kaluga

Brother Harold
and the 2002
Christian
Partner Team to
Russian

Major General
David H. Hicks,
former
Deputy Chief of
Chaplains,
U.S. Army

201

Brother Harold and Faye